Andean Common Market

Andean Common Market

Second edition

Anna Vilela Espinosa
Jorge Bernedo Alvarado

This book was originally published as a monograph in the International Encyclopaedia of Laws/Intergovernmental Organizations.

Founding Editor: Roger Blanpain
General Editor: Frank Hendrickx
Volume Editor: Jan Wouters

Wolters Kluwer

Published by:
Kluwer Law International B.V.
PO Box 316
2400 AH Alphen aan den Rijn
The Netherlands
Website: www.wolterskluwerlr.com

Sold and distributed in North, Central and South America by:
Wolters Kluwer Legal & Regulatory U.S.
7201 McKinney Circle
Frederick, MD 21704
United States of America
Email: customer.service@wolterskluwer.com

Sold and distributed in all other countries by:
Quadrant
Rockwood House
Haywards Heath
West Sussex
RH16 3DH
United Kingdom
Email: international-customerservice@wolterskluwer.com

Printed on acid-free paper

ISBN 97890-411-9055-0

e-Book: ISBN 97890-411-9061-1
web-PDF: ISBN 97890-411-9067-3

This title is available on www.kluwerlawonline.com

Printed and Bound by CPI Group (UK) Ltd, Croydon, CR0 4YY.

The Authors

Anna Vilela Espinosa was born on 17 May 1965 in Piura, Peru. She pursued her legal studies at the Universidad de Lima, Peru, from where she has a Law degree. Her Master's studies were on Labour Law and Social Security at the Universidad Nacional Mayor de San Marcos, Peru (1997–1999). She is Chief of the Labor Legal Area of AELE, member of the Research Group and Editor of ANALISIS LABORAL[1] magazine, Executive Secretary of the Asociación Peruana de Relaciones de Trabajo (APERT), member of the Sociedad Peruana de Derecho del Trabajo y de la Seguridad Social (SPDTSS), and author and co-author of numerous books and studies about Labour Law and Social Security.

1. Which has thirty nine years of publication – Luis Aparicio Valdez being its founding director and co-author of the first edition of this monography.

The Authors

Jorge Bernedo Alvarado was born in January 1948, in Ancash, Peru. He is a specialist in social research and a member of the Research Group of ANALISIS LABORAL magazine. He is a national and international consultant, author of several books and numerous articles on employment, income and poverty, social security, industrial relations, trade unionism and social security. He was the official of the United National Development Programme in Peru concerning human development from 2000 to 2009.

Table of Contents

List of Abbreviations

AC	Andean Community
ACP	Andean Competition Project
ACRI	Andean Committee on Road Infrastructure
ACTA	Andean Committee of Telecommunications Authorities
AEA	Andean Energy Alliance
AEC	Common External Tariff
AECID	Spanish Agency for International Cooperation
AFTA	Andean Free Trade Area
ALADI	Latin American Integration Association
ALALC	Latin American Association of Free Trade
APERT	Asociación Peruana de Relaciones de Trabajo
ARIAN	Andean Integrated Tariff System
BCAB	Binational Centers of Attention in Border
BIOCAN	Regional Biodiversity Programme in the Amazon
BIZ	Border Integration Zones
BPIF	Bank for Integration and Border Development Projects
CAATUR	Andean Committee of Tourism Authorities
CADS	Andean Social Development Ministers Council
CAES	Economic and Social Andean Advisory Committee
CAF	Development Bank of Latin America
CAIO	Civil Aviation International Organization
CAN	Andean Community of Nations
CANREL	Andean Committee of Electric Service Policy-Setting and Regulatory Agencies
CAPRADE	Andean Community for the Prevention and Response to Disasters
CATOCI	Andean Committee of Heads of International Cooperation Agencies of the Andean Community
CCPICAN	Advisory Council of Indigenous Peoples of the Andean
CEBAF	Binational Border Assistance Centers

List of Abbreviations

CEE	European Economic Community
CELAC	Community of Latin American and Caribbean States
CFP	Common Foreign Policy
DROSICAN	Synthetic Drugs Project of CAN
EAPAD	Andean Strategy for the Prevention and Response to Disasters
EU	European Union
FAO	Food and Agriculture Organization
FAR	Andean Reserve Fund
FDI	Foreign Direct Investment
FLAR	Latin American Reserve Fund
GEF	Global Environment Fund
GRAN	Birth of the Andean Group
GTOR	Electric Service Regulatory Agencies
ILA	Andean Labour Institute
ITU	International Telecommunication Union
JUNAC	Council of the Cartagena Agreement
	Common Southern Market
NAFTA	North American Free Trade Agreement
NANDINA	Andean Tariff Nomenclature
NBNP	List of Goods Manufactured
OANDES	Andean Social Development Objectives
OLADE	Latin American Energy Organization
OSR	Orbit Spectrum Resource
PANACEA	Andean Program Environmental Education and Communication
PIDS	Integral Plan for Social Development
SAI	Andean Integration System
SARII	South American Regional Infrastructure Integration Initiative
SEC	Community Statistic System
SGCAN	General Secretariat of the Andean Community
SIRT	Information System and Technical Regulations
SME	Small and Medium-Size Enterprise
SOCICAN	Civil Society Project
TPP	(Trans-Pacific Partnership),
UNASUR	Union of South American Nations

List of Abbreviations

UNCTAD	United Nations Conference on Trade and Development
US	United States
USD	United States Dollar
WTO	World Trade Organization

List of Abbreviations

Chapter 1. Origin and Historical Development

§1. Birth of the Andean Group (GRAN)

1. The Andean Group was established on 26 May 1969, when the heads of government of Bolivia, Colombia, Chile, Ecuador, and Peru signed the Cartagena Agreement or Subregional Agreement of Integration. This Agreement was the culmination of more than two years of uninterrupted work, investigations, and negotiations.

2. However, the idea for its creation dates back to the early 1960s, when, on 18 February 1960, various Latin American countries[1] signed the Treaty of Montevideo through which the Latin American Association of Free Trade (ALALC) was created, with the purpose of gradually abolishing internal tariffs of the signatory countries. This was the first step towards the creation of a Common Market, in which not only trade restrictions but also production factors would be gradually eliminated. Measures to coordinate and unify economic and social policies of the Member States would also be adopted. However, a short time after the creation of this Association, it became clear that, in practice, the Treaty of Montevideo favoured the most industrialized countries of the Group and did not benefit the less industrialized. Thus, the idea of uniting Bolivia, Colombia, Chile, Ecuador, Peru, and Venezuela was conceived.

3. In this context and quoting the words of Germánico Salgado,[2] the reasons that led to the constitution of the Andean Group were:

(a) The polarization of the commerce trend in major countries of ALALC.
(b) The necessity of increasing the negotiating capacity of medium and less relatively developed countries.
(c) The dissatisfaction with a very restricted integration formula based on the thesis of competition, slow and conflictive in its execution.
(d) The conviction that the basic instrument for integration shall be a common programme and policy. The countries with a relative less development within the group were the most firm supporters of programming, but all admit it as an instrument of great importance.

---

1. Mexico and the ten Latin American countries of South America.
2. Salgado, '*Ecuador and the Economic Integration of Latin America*', in *Labor Policy in the Andean Group*, ed. Luis Aparicio Valdez (BID-INTAL), 177.

(e) The attitude of the major countries in Latin America, reluctant to any fundamental modification in the Treaty of Montevideo and with the certainty that only within a group of less heterogeneous countries was it possible to find a formula to accelerate integration and avoid an unfair distribution of its fruits.

4. This being the case, on 16 August 1966, the Presidents of Colombia (Carlos Lleras), Chile (Eduardo Frei), Venezuela (Raúl Leoni) and former President of Ecuador (Galo Plaza), and Chancellor (Fernando Schwalb) of Peru, appointed as delegates for the Presidents of Ecuador and Peru respectively, signed the Declaration of Bogota, in which they pointed out that it was necessary to give a new orientation to the process of Latin American integration. Thus, they decided to 'go forward with a joint action within the framework of ALALC, in order to achieve the adoption of practical formulae to accelerate the progress of the countries with less relative economic development and insufficient trade'.[3]

5. Afterwards, and based on the Declaration of Bogota, the Declaration of the Presidents of South America was signed on 14 April 1967 in Punta del Este, Uruguay, in which the decision to promote the gradual creation of a Latin American Common Market was proclaimed.

6. A Commission comprising representatives from Colombia, Ecuador, Chile, Peru, and Venezuela was set up, with the purpose of studying the establishment of the subregional integration group that had been subscribed to in the Declaration of Bogotá, and to carry out the corresponding negotiations as well. On 16 August 1967, Bolivia joined this Commission. Afterwards the Council of Ministers of the Latin American Integration Association (ALADI) approved Resolution 202, in which the principals that would enforce the norms of the subregional agreements were set up, and Resolution 203 containing the basis of a subregional agreement between Bolivia, Colombia, Chile, Ecuador, Peru, and Venezuela. The above-mentioned Commission had six meetings; the last one was in May 1969 in Cartagena de Indias, Colombia, where a definitive agreement was reached by the representatives of Bolivia, Colombia, Chile, Ecuador, and Peru.

§2. Historical Evolution of the Andean Group

I. Basis of the Subregional Andean Integration, 1969–1979

7. The Cartagena Agreement was signed at the Palacio de San Carlos, in Bogota, Colombia, on 26 May 1969.

Five countries signed the Agreement through their representatives: Tomás Guillermo Elio for Bolivia, Jorge Valencia Jaramillo for Colombia, Salvador Lluch Soler for Chile, José Pons Vizcaíno for Ecuador, and Vicente Cerro Cebrián for Peru. Venezuela did not sign the Agreement although it had taken part in all the negotiations.

---

3. Andean Community. General Secretariat, *28 Years of Andean Integration. A Historical Recount*, 8.

8. Even though the Cartagena Agreement, signed on 26 May 1969, was declared compatible with the Treaty of Montevideo, and with the general principles of Resolution 203 and Resolution 202, it was not enforced until 16 October of the same year, when it was officially ratified by the government of Peru. It had already been ratified by the governments of Colombia and Chile. With Peru's ratification, the requisite in Article 110° of the Agreement that it could only start operating when 'three countries had communicated their approval to the Executive Secretary of the ALALC' was fulfilled. The Cartagena Agreement was ratified afterwards by Ecuador and Bolivia in November 1969.

9. Activities officially started on 21 November 1969 with the installation in Lima of the Commission, the highest body in the Cartagena Agreement. Three days later, the Foreign Affairs Ministers of Bolivia, Colombia, Chile, Ecuador, and Peru designated this city as the permanent headquarters of the Board of the Cartagena Agreement. In 1973, as a result of a series of negotiations that began with the installation of the Commission, Venezuela joined the Agreement with the same rights and obligations as Colombia, Chile and Peru. In 1976, Chile withdrew from the Agreement.

10. The principal organizations that existed since the beginnings were the above-mentioned Cartagena Agreement Commission and the Council of the Cartagena Agreement (JUNAC), the technical body of the process. There was also an auxiliary body, the Economic and Social Andean Advisory Committee (CAES).

Special mention should be made of the Andean Development Corporation (CAF), a financial institution created months before the signing of the Cartagena Agreement.

11. Once progress had been made in the integration process, the Andean institutional structure was reinforced with new specialized bodies that were responsible for specific areas of interest. Thus, three Agreements were created, known as Social Agreements: the Andres Bello Agreement in January 1970, to promote education; the Hipólito Unanue Agreement in December 1971, to promote integration in the health sector; the Simón Rodríguez Agreement, in October 1973, to improve living and working conditions in the subregion.

12. The Andean Reserve Fund (FAR) was founded in 1976, a financial institution that in 1991 became the Latin American Reserve Fund (FLAR). Three new organizations were created by the end of the 1970s. The Creation Treaty signed on 28 May 1979, starting activities in 1984; the Andean Parliament created on 25 October 1979; and The Andean Council of Foreign Affairs Ministers created on 12 November 1979, aimed at directing the external action of the various organizations of integration.

13. Among others, the Andean Business Advisory Council (Decision 175, 1983) and the Andean Labour Advisory Council (Decision 176, 1983) were created. A resolution proposing a training centre, investigation, broadcasting and council that would facilitate the effective participation of the workers in the process of integration, aid the work executed by the Council and help with the activities carried out by national unions, was adopted in the second meeting of the latter body. The establishment of the Andean Labour Institute (ILA) stemming from a study carried out and based on an agreement between the European Economic Community (CEE) and the Cartagena Agreement was the next step.[4]

14. The Cartagena Agreement was aimed at promoting a balanced and harmonious development in the Member Countries, by means of integration, economic, and social cooperation, accelerating growth through economic integration, facilitating participation in the process of regional integration stipulated in the Treaty of Montevideo, and establishing favourable conditions to convert the ALALC into a Common Latin American Market.

15. The application of certain techniques which would be the core of its principal actions was taken into account by the Agreement. These were basically: a gradual harmonization of social and economic policies, a Programme of Trade Liberalization through the establishment of an Andean Zone of free trade, and the adoption of a Common External Tariff (AEC).

16. It was also agreed that to complement the mechanisms mentioned previously, the following programmes and actions of social and economic cooperation would be promoted: external actions in the economic field on matters of common interest, programmes aimed to spur scientific and technological development, actions in the field of border integration, programmes in the tourism area, actions for the utilization and conservation of natural resources and environment, programmes in services and social development, and actions in social communication.

17. The process of policy harmonization established in the Cartagena Agreement had to be accomplished at the same time and in coordination with the Subregional Common Market through the application of mechanisms such as: a joint industrial programme, with the approval of sector programmes of industrial development, which would be carried out jointly with the Member Countries; a special regime for the agriculture and cattle raising sector; planning for physical and social infrastructure; harmonization of monetary, fiscal, and financial policies; application of a common trade policy; and the harmonization of planning methods and techniques.

18. The necessary procedures to enforce the above-mentioned mechanisms, established before 31 December 1970, are: a Common Regime on Foreign Capital, Brands, Patents, Licenses and Exemptions, and a Uniform Regime for Multinational Andean Enterprises. On 31 December 1972, a programme to harmonize the instruments and mechanisms of the regulation of foreign trade in the Member Countries was also put into practice.

19. The Andean integration process also considered, as we have already pointed out, the creation of an Andean Free Trade Zone. To achieve this purpose, a Programme of Liberalization was established with the objective of eliminating duties and restrictions on imports from any Member Country. It would be automatic and irrevocable, comprising all products and ending with total liberalization by 31 December 1980. It would also establish that all sorts of restrictions for the intra-subregional trade would be eliminated by 31 December 1970, although Bolivia and Ecuador could carry out these actions later.

---

4. This bilateral programme was jointly carried out by the Italian advisor Arpes with the consultant called by the JUNAC, Dr Luis Aparicio Valdez & Morgado V. Emilio, *Study on Andean Socio-Labor Integration. Specially the Simon Rodriguez Agreement* (Lima, Peru: Aele Mayo, 1999).

20. The products were grouped in lists, including a List of Exceptions to the Liberalization Programme.

However, due to the fact that each list had its own deadlines and forms of tax exemptions, and taking into account that its application differed in the case of the less-developed countries (Colombia, Peru, Venezuela) or relatively less-developed (Bolivia and Ecuador), the realization of this programme suffered some complications, although there were some promising advances during the early years, and tax exemptions were achieved in some cases. Consequently, the deadlines that had been established in the Cartagena Agreement were not always met, so it was necessary to extend them. This was done through the Protocols of Lima in 1976 and Arequipa in 1978.

21. In regard to the elimination of all the restrictions according to Article 46° of the Cartagena Agreement, Colombia, Peru, and Venezuela made important advances in this respect. Bolivia and Ecuador made limited ones.

22. Another mechanism in the Cartagena Agreement was the adoption, in two stages, of an AEC. A Minimum External Tariff was approved at the end of 1970, stipulating that no national tariff could be set below it, this being only partially enforced since it was not compulsory for Bolivia and Ecuador and it did not include all custom duties. In the same way, the Member Countries committed themselves to an AEC by 31 December 1973, which would be approved by the Commission within two years. The Member Countries would then begin an annual process starting on 31 December 1976 to AEC, culminating in its enforcement on 30 December 1980.

II. The 1980s

23. The advances achieved by the Andean Group in the 1970s were interrupted at the beginning of the 1980s due to external factors such as the international financial crisis, the foreign debt and internal factors related to national economic policies and, in some cases, natural disasters:

> The impulse of the process was drastically restrained in terms of trade; restrictions were applied unilaterally by countries, thereby curtailing the advances already accomplished in the liberalization program; the economic operators saw the rules of the game, that had made them take advantage of an extended subregional market, abruptly changed; integration became marginal within the countries priorities of economic development; the initial ideas of harmonization remained paralyzed and the definition of a common external tariff was not carried out.[5]

24. Due to these difficulties and with the impossibility of accomplishing the established commitments, the Council – the technical body of the process – and the Commission – the organization that approves its decisions – began actions to modify the Agreement in order to make it adequate for the new reality in the Andean countries. Thus, in May 1987, the Modifying Protocol of Quito was signed and served to maintain the harmonization of the economic policies, and the mechanisms and basic instruments

5. Vieira Posada, *The Extended Andean Market: A reality* (Colombia: Chamber of Commerce of Bogota, April 1999), 24.

to accomplish an Andean Customs Union; the deadlines and established ways to achieve them were modified.

25. This Protocol has been criticized for its wide flexibility with regard to commercial commitments, such as, the postponement of dates to finish the exemptions list and not giving the exact date for the establishing of the AEC. What is worth mentioning is that 'this instrument contributed to the reactivation of the process, by lifting the unilateral restrictions and channelling the unfulfilled commitments within the juridical norms in the Agreement'.[6]

III. Adaptation to World Changes

26. Towards the end of the 1980s, a series of changes and transformations took place at the international level. They were the result of globalization and the opening up of the economy and led to an attempt to change an inward-looking Andean subregional integration process into a scheme of open regionalism.

27. Starting from 1989, the direct intervention of the Andean presidents in the process of integration sped up trade liberalization. Three successive acts were subscribed to in this period, such as the Galápagos Act (December 1989), with two important objectives: (i) to consolidate the Andean economic area and improve its political say within the international context and (ii) to reinforce its contribution to Latin American unity; the La Paz Act (November 1990), that proposed the acceleration of the Andean Common Market structure for 1995, thus culminating in the total liberalization of intra-subregional trade and establishing an AEC with the harmonization of economic policies related to foreign trade at the same time; the Barahona Act (December 1991), that launched a concrete programme to form the Free Trade Zone and the adoption of AEC, pointing out specific directions for the institutional transformation of the Andean Group (GRAN).

28. In August 1992, the Commission of the Cartagena Agreement approved Decision 324 through which Bolivia, Colombia, Ecuador, and Venezuela agreed with the process of the formation of the Free Trade Zone that would be completed on 30 September of the same year, eliminating duties for products that, up to that date, were still subject to duty in those countries.

In the case of Ecuador, and in order to eliminate 75% of its existing duty on the imports from Venezuela, it was established that 50% should be eliminated on 30 September 1992 and the other 50% on 31 January 1993.

29. The Free Trade Zone of GRAN started to function in Bolivia, Colombia, Ecuador, and Venezuela in February 1993. The situation was different in Peru. After difficult years and long discussions, Peru and the other members of the Andean Community (AC) reached an agreement for the total incorporation of that country to the Free Trade Zone. Thus, through Decision 414, the Commission approved the Duties Exemption Agenda on Tariff Exemptions, which came into effect on 1 August 1997 and should end in 2005.

30. From then on, and until the adoption of the Protocol of Sucre in 1977, the GRAN was affected by a paradoxical situation:

6. Vieira Posada, *supra* n. 6, 27.

on one hand, the intra-subregional trade followed an upward trend – it reached $4705 millions in 1996, an increase of more than 250% respect 1992 (…) – but, on the other hand, the negotiations in the Cartagena Agreement Commission could not solve neither technically nor juridically the incorporation of Perú into the Free Trade Zone, nor the formulation of the Common External Tariff, essential instrument for the creation of the Customs Union and agreements about criteria for the harmonization of macroeconomic policies were not achieved. This brought about a significant setback in the consolidation of the Free Trade Zone.[7]

IV. A New Institutional Framework: Creation of the AC

31. The need to give a new impulse to the process of Andean integration arose from the fact that although the Andean institution in operation could accomplish the objectives in the Cartagena Agreement, it could not face tasks of a more advanced process of integration, such as those of the Common Market.

32. Consequently, by means of the Modifying Protocol of the Andean Subregional Integration Agreement (Cartagena Agreement), agreed to on the occasion of the VIIIth meeting of the Andean Presidential Council in Trujillo, on 10 March 1996 and in effect since June 1997, institutional reforms were introduced in the Cartagena Agreement and the Andean Community – with headquarters in Lima, Peru – and the Andean Integration System (SAI) was created with the objective of providing a solid, modern, and flexible institution with high political backing to aid the process of Andean Integration.

33. New regulations tending to reconcile the Modifying Protocol of the Court of Justice with the recently approved Protocol were established to strengthen the Andean Parliament; promote the shareholding of the Andean Development Corporation; fortify the Andrés Bello, Hipólito Unanue, Simón Rodríguez agreements and the José Celestino Mutis Programme; and direct the regulatory framework for the establishment, operation and use of Andean satellites by multinational companies and others, for the strengthening of the AC's external actions.[8]

34. Notwithstanding that the Protocol of Trujillo institutionally consolidated the Andean Group, the problem remained of Peru's total incorporation into the group, making it necessary to achieve a solution. Thus, in December 1996, the Member Countries granted Peru time to deliberate its total incorporation into the Free Trade Zone.

During that time, negotiations were difficult, thus ending with the announcement of the withdrawal of Peru from the Andean Group.

35. The Protocol of Sucre was subscribed to on June 1997. It is responsible for incorporating the modifications to the Cartagena Agreement that aimed at solving the crisis that the Andean Group was undergoing and establishing new regulations recognizing the changes in the process of integration and globalization at regional and international levels. Accordingly, some articles of the Agreement of Cartagena were

7. Maldonado Lira, *30 Years of Andean Integration Balance and Perspective* (Lima, Peru: Andean Community. General Secretariat, 1999), 97.
8. Maldonado Lira, *supra* n. 8, 112.

modified or removed, namely those that had become obsolete and that were related to the Programme of Liberalization, the AEC (putting an end to the Common Minimum External Tariff as a first step towards the incorporation of the AEC), the programmes of industrial integration, and the agreements on industrial complementation.

36. Three new chapters were also added to the Cartagena Agreement. One chapter was about external affairs. It established that the Andean Council of Foreign Affairs Ministers would be responsible for the foreign policy common to the members and would organize common political positions to achieve joint participation in fora and international political organizations.

This body would define, along with the Andean Community Commission, a common strategy to strengthen Andean integration with the rest of the regional economic processes and their relation in the political, social, and economic-commercial scene to the extra-regional schemes.

37. The second chapter incorporated deals with intra-subregional services trade in which, as proposed by the General Secretariat, the Andean Community Commission would approve a general framework of principles and regulations to achieve the liberalization of the intra-subregional services trade. The third chapter dealt with associate members, allowing the AC to receive associate members with great flexibility. To accomplish this, the Andean Council of Foreign Affairs Ministers could grant associate member status to a country agreeing to a Free Trade Treaty with the Member Countries. This would have to be preceded by a proposal of the Andean Community Commission.

38. Regarding the Peruvian situation, it was established that, notwithstanding Article 75 of the Cartagena Agreement, the Andean Community Commission would define the terms of the Liberalization Program to be applied to Peru and the rest of the Member Countries, with the aim of achieving the Andean Free Trade Zone by 31 December 2005. At the same time, regulations of the Andean Council of Foreign Affairs Ministers and the General Secretariat were approved in Decisions 407 and 409, and the election of the Secretary General of the AC in Decision 408.

39. In April 1998, during the Xth Andean Presidential Council, an evaluation of the development of the Andean subregional integration process was carried out and the Act of Guayaquil was signed.

The Act contains a series of regulations to guide the process.

40. In 2003, through the 'Declaración of Quirama', a social dimension was included into the Andean subregional integration process, and the Integral Plan for Social Development (PIDS) was developed through a presidential mandate.

41. In 2004, several CAN (Andean Community of Nations) institutions were created: the Andean Council of Education Ministers and Principals in charge of the Cultural Policies (Decision 593); the Andean Council of Social Development Ministers (Decision 592); the Andean Community's Council of Environmental and Sustainable Development Ministers (Decision 596); the Andean Advisory Council of Municipal Authorities (Decision 585).

42. During the same year, the South American Community of Nations was created politically during the Third South American Presidential Summit, held in Cusco, Perú, and the Andean Council of Foreign Ministers approved Chile's request to participate as an Observer in the Andean Community.

43. One year later, the AC and the European Union (EU) initiated the joint assessment of the Andean integration process, so as to enable a future association between the two blocs that would include a Free Trade Agreement.

44. The Andean Council of Foreign Ministers, meeting in an enlarged session with the CAN Commission through Decision 613, granted the status of Associate Membership to Argentina, Brazil, Paraguay, and Uruguay (countries which integrate MERCOSUR), and so the Andean Advisory Council of Municipal Authorities was installed.

45. In 2006, Peru culminated the tariff reduction process, as foreseen in Decision 414, thereby completing its full incorporation into the Andean Free Trade Area (AFTA), and for the first time chose its representatives to the Andean Parliament through direct, universal, and secret elections.

During that same year, the Andean Council of Foreign Ministers approved Decision 633, which equated the number of judges of the Andean Community Court of Justice with the number of CAN Member Countries (4). Afterwards, through Decision 666, Chile was incorporated as an Associate Member Country in the Andean Community.

46. In the course of the Seventeen Andean Council of Presidents, held in Tarija, Bolivia, which took place in 2007, the presidents of all the Member Countries of the Andean Community agreed to commence with an integration, which would initiate a more balanced approach between the social aspect and the cultural, economical, political, environmental, and commercial ones.

Likewise, the negotiations between the AC and the EU started in order to establish an Association Agreement based on three main pillars: Political Dialogue, Cooperation, and Commerce.

47. On the other hand, in order to promote the active participation of the indigenous communities in subregional integration matters, the Consultative Council of the Andean Community Indigenous People was established as a consultative body within the framework of the Andean Integration System.

48. During 2008, various projects were realized. Thus, the Regional Biodiversity Programme in the Amazon (BIOCAN Programme), an initiative of the CAN Member Countries and General Secretariat was launched with the support of Government of Finland. This project sought the conservation and sustainable use of the Amazon area of the Andean countries.

Since the beginning the projects (Synthetic Drugs Project of CAN (DROSICAN) and (Civil Society Project (SOCICAN)) were aimed at various civil society actors.

Some collective communal standards were approved, some of which regulate issues such as sanitary regulations, quality control, the vigilance of products regarding domestic hygiene and personal absorbents, among others.

49. In 2009, a series of communal standards and several programmes were carried out. Thus, it was in order to protect the health of the Andean citizens through Decision 721 that the requirements were approved for establishments manufacturing products of domestic hygiene and absorbent personal hygiene products in the Andean region.

50. In February 2010, the Andean Council of Foreign Ministers, meeting in an enlarged session with the Commission, approved certain guidelines that would lead the Andean integration process as well as the Strategic Agenda with twelve lines of consensus; therefore, the promotion and diffusion of the Andean integration as well as the diversity of the cultural and natural wealth of the subregion, through modern means and the use of technology in communication and information, was formalized and given impetus through Decision 739. The role of the observer country of the CAN was also adopted through Decision 741.

51. Citizens of the four Member Countries of the Andean Community finally began using the Andean Passport when Colombia embarked upon this expedition, with similar characteristics to those of Bolivia, Ecuador, and Peru.

On that same year, the General Secretariat of the CAN and the International Organization for Migration signed an agreement in order to spread the communal norms regarding migratory issues, and the Andean Council of Foreign Ministers declared 2011 as the 'Year of Andean Social Integration'.

52. In 2011, Spain officially requested to be a CAN Observer, which would enable it to promote programmes, joint actions, and to participate and rightfully voice opinion on meetings held by the Andean Community.

53. On the latter, the VII declaration of the Andean Council of Ministers of Social Development was signed in Lima, Peru, which approved eleven Andean Social Development Objectives (OANDES) and their corresponding targets, which they pledged to achieve by 2019, together with an Andean Economic and Social Cohesion Strategy comprising priority activities as well as their respective lines of action.

54. On 28 July 2011, the Presidential Declaration of Lima was signed in the city of Lima at the XVIIIth Andean Presidential Council, expressing the commitment to strengthen and give renewed momentum to the Andean integration process, convinced that it makes important contributions to Latin American integration, as well as the agreement of the Member Countries on the need to embark upon a revision of the institutional structure and operation of the Andean Integration System. It also hailed the transfer of the Pro Tempore Presidency of the Andean Community for the period 2011–2012 to the Republic of Colombia.

55. In August 2011, during the XXXII meeting of the Andean Council of Foreign Affairs, the ministers of the Member Countries of the CAN adopted seven community standards that strengthen the CAN in the areas of civic participation, environment, cooperation, and external relations.

56. Through Decision 758, the Bureau of peoples of African descent of the Andean Community, as a consultative body in the context of the SAI, was established in order to promote the active participation of the representatives' organizations of this sector in the matters related to subregional integration.

57. Another Decision taken was Decision 759 (August 2011), which outlined Andean Strategy to improve the effectiveness of the International Development Cooperation, under the Andean Strategic Agenda and the principles of the Paris Declaration, with the aim of strengthening the management and coordination of cooperation.

58. By Decision 760, the Andean Council of Ministers of Culture and Cultures to be responsible for recommending, designing, defining, and monitoring Andean cultural policies was created, and by Decision 761, the Foreign Ministers of the CAN gave Spain the status of Observer country of the CAN, with a voice but no vote.

59. Through Decision 762, Foreign Ministers approved the project *Programme for Adaptation to Climate Change in the Andean Region*, with the emphasis on small producers.

60. Decision 763 approved the *Andean Strategy for Integrated Water Resources Management,* which aims to promote joint action for development, sustainability, and strengthening of the Integrated Management of Water Resources in Member Countries of the Andean Community.

61. Likewise, the Andean Council of Foreign Affairs Ministers endorsed the signing of the cooperation project between Food and Agriculture Organization (FAO) and General Secretariat of the Andean Community (SGCAN) through Decision 764, for the strengthening of subregional control of Classical Swine Fever in the Andean countries. The implementation of the project was already approved by the Commission through Decision 754, in order to support the Agricultural Health Services Officers of the countries in the Control and Eradication of Classical Swine Fever. This transboundary disease is considered of major importance for swine, for losses caused to the countries of the region.

62. Decision 760 created the Andean Council of Ministers of Culture and Cultures, which was responsible for recommending, designing, defining, and monitoring Andean cultural policies.

To implement these community standards, the Andean Committee on Cultural Industries and the Andean Committee for Cultural Heritage Material and Immaterial were created, which add to the already existing Andean Committee for Combating Illicit Trafficking of Cultural Property.

63. Through Decision 766 (7 December 2011) the Consolidated Text of the Common Nomenclature of Andean Countries based on harmonized commodity description and coding system called 'Nandina' is approved, to ease the identification and classification of goods, statistics of foreign trade, and other trade policy measures of the Andean Community relating to the import and export of goods.

64. Decision 771 regarding the Tariff Policy of the Andean Community extended until 31 December 2014, the deadlines specified in Articles 1, 2 and 3 of Decision 695.

65. On 6 November 2012 through Decision 778, the Decision 574 titled 'Andean Customs Control Regime' was replaced.

66. The update and creation of statistical records systems in the Member Countries of the SAI was issued through Decision 780 dated 11 March 2013. Through this Decision, the basis for the statistics development are established based on statistical records in the Member Countries of the Andean Community, setting standards in order to create and update a system of statistical records.

67. By Decision 792 dated 19 September 2013, the implementation of Reengineering the Andean Integration System was decided. For this purpose the creation of a High-Level Group level is set. This group will: (a) Review the Andean Integration System in order to adapt to new realities and challenges in the international context; (b) Start the process of preparing a protocol to facilitate the departure of the Andean Parliament from the Integration System, the same that once signed would be subject to approval by the legislatures of the Member Countries; (c) Analyse more precisely and efficiently the relationship that the Andean Community has with three major entities that were created by the CAN and are the Andean Development Corporation, the FLAR, and the Andean Health Organization.

68. Through Decision 794 dated 13 and 19 September 2013, the amendments to the Consolidated Text of the NANDINA were approved, in order to facilitate the identification and classification of goods. This decision came into force on 1 January 2014 and had as deadline for implementation 1 July 2014, for countries that require it.

69. Decision 797 dated 14 October 2014 through which the relationship of the committees and ad hoc groups of the Andean Community that are related directly with the guidelines and areas of priority action in the framework of Decision 792 was approved. This Decision concerns the implementation of the reengineering of the Andean Integration System.

70. The CAN Commission approved Decision 798 on 5 November 2014, which updates the Common Tariff Nomenclature of the Member Countries of the Andean Community, NANDINA, based on the Harmonized Commodity Description, and Coding of the World Customs Organization (WCO). The CAN Commission also approved on 19 February 2015 Decision 799, which provides that the customs authorities of the importing Member Country will not prevent the clearance of the goods when a product is included in the nomenclature of goods not manufactured in the Subregion, delinking the process of certifying and control of origin certificates of that list.

71. Through Decision 802 dated 19 December 2014, the deadline that empowers the Member Countries to temporarily suspend the execution of Decision 436 is extended, which was amended by Decisions 684, 767, 785, and Resolution 630 of the General Secretariat.

72. On 24 April 2015 through Decision 803, were approved the provisions related to the General Framework of Principles and Provisions for Liberalizing Trade in Services in the Andean Community.

73. Through Decision 805, dated 24 April 2015, regarding the tariff policy of the Andean Community Decisions 370, 465, and 535 and those that may replace, amend, or supplement on the AEC are rendered null.

Chapter 2. Present Institutional Framework: The Andean Community and the Andean Integration System

74. A new impetus was given to Andean subregional integration when the Protocol of Trujillo was signed and came into effect in 1977, creating the Andean Community and the institution of the SAI.

75. The aim of the Andean Integration System is to allow effective coordination of its bodies and institutions, to intensify Andean subregional integration, promote its external presence, and consolidate actions related to the process of integration.[9]

76. In this context, Chapter II of the Cartagena Agreement, which referred to the bodies of the Agreement, was substituted with one that deals with the Andean Community, and SAI. The main0020changes to this chapter were: the incorporation of the Andean Presidential Council, and the Andean Council of Foreign Affairs Ministers in the Andean Juridical order; changes in the Commission structure; and the creation of the General Secretariat of the Community. Afterwards, the reforms to the Court of Justice were carried out through the Protocol Modifying Charter, signed on 28 May 1996. Other bodies had been submitted to process according to the Protocol of Trujillo. Thus, for example, as in the case of the Andean Parliament, an Additional Protocol that grants direct election to its representatives has been signed.

77. The Andean Integration System is now comprised of the following bodies and institutions, which were mainly created within the first ten years of the process:

- Andean Presidential Council (Highest Body);
- Andean Council of Foreign Affairs Ministers (Direction and Decision-Making Bodies);
- Commission of the Andean Community (Direction and Decision-Making Bodies);
- General Secretariat of the Andean Community (Technical Support and Executive Body);
- Court of Justice of the Andean Community (Jurisdictional Body);
- Andean Parliament (Deliberative Body);
- Andean Business Advisory Council (Consultative Institution of SAI);
- Andean Labour Advisory Council (Consultative Institution of SAI);
- Consultative Council of the Indigenous People (Consultative Institution of SAI);
- Consultative Council of Municipal Authorities (Consultative Institution of SAI);

9. *Andean Informative*, No. 9, May 1996 (*Andean Newsletter*).

- Andean Development Corporation (Financial Institution);
- Latin American Reserve Fund (Financial Institution);
- Simon Rodriguez Agreement, and the Andean Health Organization Hipólito Unanue Agreement (Social Agreements);
- Simon Bolivar Andean University (Educational Institution);

and

- All other bodies and institutions to be created in the framework of the Andean Subregional integration.

78. The Andean Presidential Council was created on 23 May 1990 during a meeting of the Andean leaders, which was celebrated in Macchu Picchu, Cusco, Peru. It is the highest body of the SAI, which is comprised by the Presidents of the Member Countries responsible for defining policy on Andean integration and issuing guidelines about different spheres of responsibility and mechanisms established in their respective Treaties or Constitutive Instruments. Its President holds the highest political office in the Andean Community, finding himself in charge of: convoking and presiding over all ordinary meeting as well as all extraordinary ones held by the council; executing the council's and the Andean community's representation; supervising the withholding of compliance of all the other organs and institutions of the SAI and the guidelines, which are produced by the council, and holding the position for one calendar year. This position is then filled in alphabetical order by each of the Member Countries.

79. The Council meets once a year, preferably in the country that exercises its Presidency. It evaluates the actions carried out by bodies and institutions of SAI, its plans, programmes, and suggestions. It may meet in a special session any time it deems it advisable.

80. The Council's functions are: to define the Andean subregional integration policy; to orient and initiate actions on all matters of interest to the subregion as a whole, as well as the relative coordination within the organs and institutions of the SAI; to evaluate the development and the results of the process of the subregional integration process and its external projection among others.

81. The Andean Council of Foreign Affairs Ministers, created on 12 November 1979, is a political body responsible for achieving the Andean subregional integration objectives, its main function being the issuing and executing of foreign policies of the Member Countries in affairs that are of subregional interest, for example, as it is to orient and coordinate the external action of the diverse organs and institutions of the SAI. Moreover, it is responsible for, and carries out and evaluates, the general policies of the Andean subregional integration process in coordination with the Commission.

82. Furthermore, it is in charge of complying with the guidelines imparted by the Andean Presidential Council and also ensuring that all other guidelines directed to other organs and institutions of the SAI are withheld; signing conventions and agreements on global foreign policies and cooperation issues with countries or groups of countries or with international organizations. It also coordinates the joint position of the Member Countries in international fora and international matters within its sphere of competition.

83. The Andean Council of Foreign Affairs Ministers is presided over by the Foreign Relations Minister of the country in charge of the Presidency of the Andean Presidential Council, who will remain for one year in that position/charge, and integrated by the Ministers of Foreign Affairs of the Member Countries, who are permanent plenipotentiaries. They engage in necessary matters and deal with all pertinent issues before the Council. When it meets in enlarged sessions, the Council is also comprised of the representatives of the Commission in order to consider matters of interest to both bodies. It usually meets twice a year, preferably in the country that exercises the Presidency of its Council, and at any other time it deems it advisable. The Council has the legislative capacity in the matters of foreign policy and expresses its will through Declarations (which are in fact manifestations of a non-binding character) and Decisions, the latter being part of the juridical order of the Andean Community.

84. The Commission of the Andean Community is the policy-making body of the SAI with legislative capacity, expressed in the adoption of Decisions, shared now with the Andean Council of Foreign Affairs Ministers.[10] The Commission is responsible for issuing, carrying out, and evaluating Andean subregional integration of trade and investment matters. It also adopts, in coordination with the Andean Council of Foreign Affairs Ministers, when necessary, the necessary steps to accomplish the objectives of the Cartagena Agreement and to fulfil the Guidelines of the Andean Presidential Council.

85. The Commission is comprised of a plenipotentiary representative of each of the governments of the Member Countries. Each government appoints a titular and an alternate representative. It usually meets three times a year or when summoned by its President. Their meetings take place in the seat of the General Secretariat although they may take place elsewhere in the Andean Area.

86. The General Secretariat is the executive body of the Andean Community and, as such, acts only on behalf of the subregional interests, giving technical and executive support, when necessary, to the other bodies and institutions of SAI. According to Article 30° of the Cartagena Agreement, it is responsible for observing that the Cartagena Agreement and the norms and regulations that comprise the juridical order of the Andean Community are carried out. It works on the recommendations of the Andean Council of Foreign Affairs Ministers and the Commission and submits decisions to their respective bodies. It also takes suggestions and initiatives to the meeting of the Andean Council of Foreign Ministers to facilitate or accelerate the keeping of the Agreement in order to achieve its objectives in the shortest possible term.

87. The Secretariat is a permanent body and its headquarters are in Lima, Peru. It expresses its will through Resolutions, and it is comprised of a General Secretary – chosen by consensus by the Andean Council of Foreign Affairs Ministers in extended meeting with the Commission – General Directors, and technical and administrative staff.

88. The Court of Justice is the judicial body of the Andean Community, which is comprised of four Judges. They must be native citizens of the Member Countries and are appointed in sets of three by each Member Country and by a unanimous vote of the plenipotentiaries assigned for that purpose. It ensures the legality of the community norms. It also interprets the regulations that comprise the Juridical Order of the Andean

10. Article 3° of the Cartagena Agreement.

Community, to ensure they are applied uniformly among the Member Countries, and settles disputes with regard to omission or failure of the Member Countries to fulfil their obligations. Has territorial jurisdiction in the four countries, with permanent headquarters in Quito, Ecuador.

89. The Treaty of the Creation of the Court of Justice was modified by the Protocol of Cochabamba signed on 28 May 1996, assigning the following additional powers:

(a) It may rule on a Petition for Omission or Failure to Act, by which Member Countries, legal entities or natural persons, the Andean Council of Foreign Affairs Ministers, the Commission, or the General Secretariat can start a lawsuit against when the latter three organs fail to fulfil their duties as established by the Andean Judicial Law.
(b) The Arbitrary Capacity, by which the Court serves as Arbitrator over disputes that ensue between SAI bodies and institutions or private persons, when the parties agree to that procedure.
(c) Labour Jurisdiction, through which it is competent to rule on labour disputes that arise in the SAI bodies and institutions.

90. Its new bylaws, which update and detail the procedures carried out in this court, were approved on 22 June 2011 by the Andean Council of Foreign Ministers.

91. The Andean Parliament is the deliberative body of the Andean Subregion Integration System; it has a communitarian nature and represents the peoples of the Andean Community. It has international juridical capacity.

92. According to its Constitutive Treaty[11] it has competence to:

(a) Participate in putting forward and guiding the Process of the Andean Subregional Integration to achieve the consolidation of Latin American integration.
(b) Examine the progress of the Process of Andean Subregional Integration and the accomplishment of its objectives by requiring periodical reports from the bodies and institutions of the Andean Integration System.
(c) Issue budget recommendations to the bodies and institutions of the Andean Integration System of Projects, which are made up of contributions from the Member Countries.
(d) Suggest actions or decisions regarding adoption of modifications, adjustments, or new general guidelines with relation to the planned objectives and the institutional structure of the Andean Integration System.
(e) Participate in the rule-making process through suggestions to the bodies of the Andean Integration System that deal with Projects of Regulations, about matters of common interest that can be incorporated to the juridical order of the Andean Community.
(f) Promote harmonization of legislations in the Member Countries.
(g) Promote cooperation and coordination with the Parliaments of Member Countries, Bodies and Institutions of the Andean Integration System, and the other Parliamentary Bodies of Integration or Cooperation with other countries.

11. Modified in Sucre, Bolivia, on 23 Apr. 1997.

93. The Parliament is comprised of representatives of the National Congresses, in accordance with their internal regulations and the General Regulations of the Parliament. They are elected by direct universal suffrage – in the case of Ecuador and Peru, its representatives were elected by this way – by the following bodies: the Assembly, the Directive Board, the Commissions, and Secretariats and Offices. It holds two Sessions annually. Its permanent seat is in Santa Fe de Bogota, Colombia.

94. The Andean Business and Labour Advisory Councils are advisory institutions of the Andean Integration System, comprised of top-level delegates. Both the Business Advisory and the Labour Advisory Councils are responsible for issuing their opinions on programmes or activities of the subregional integration process that are of interest to their respective sectors. These opinions are brought before the Andean Council of Foreign Affairs Ministers, the Commission, or the SGCAN, upon request or on their own initiative.

95. They can also be summoned to workshops and governmental experts' meetings, related to the elaboration of projects and can participate in Commission meetings.

96. The Consultative Council of the Andean Community Indigenous People was established by Decision 674, as a consultative body within the framework of the Andean Integration System. The functions and competencies of this Council are the same as consultative bodies of entrepreneurs and workers of SAI. Thus, it can issue opinions to the Andean Council of Foreign Affairs Ministers, the Commission, or the SGCAN and attend meetings of government experts or working groups related to their activities.

97. It is also responsible for promoting the exchange, evaluation, and dissemination of successful experiences and practices, institutional strengthening and promoting cooperation among people and indigenous organizations, government entities, and agencies of human rights and civil society of the Andean subregion.

98. The Development Bank of Latin America (CAF) is a financial institution of SAI established in 1970 and currently comprises eighteen countries in Latin America, the Caribbean, and Europe, as well as fourteen private banks in the Andean region. Its mission is to spur the Andean Subregional Integration process and support the sustainable development of its shareholder countries through an efficient use of funds for the timely delivery of multiple financial services to public and private clients.

99. The CAF is headquartered in Caracas, Venezuela, and its main functions are to: (a) carry out studies to identify direct investment opportunities and develop appropriate projects; (b) disseminate among the Andean countries the results of their research and studies in order to properly direct the investment of available resources; (c) provide directly or indirectly technical and financial assistance for the preparation and execution of multinational projects or complementary; (d) obtain internal and external loans; (e) issue bonds, debentures and other obligations, which may be placed inside or outside of shareholder countries, among others.[12]

100. The CAF is comprised of Latin American and Caribbean investors. Its main associates are Argentina, Costa Rica, Spain, Chile, Brazil, Mexico, Paraguay, República Dominicana, Trinidad and Tobago, Panama, Uruguay, and fifteen private banks in the Andean region.

---

12. *Andean Newsletter*, No. 11, *supra* .

101. The FLAR was born in November 1976 as an extension of the FAR. This is a financial institution whose purpose is to provide balance of payments assistance to the Member Countries by granting credits or guaranteeing loans to third parties. It also helps harmonize the countries' exchange, monetary and financial policies, and improves the terms of investments of international reserves made by the Andean countries.

102. Its objectives are to: support the balance of payments of Member Countries by granting loans or guaranteeing third-party loans; improve the conditions of international reserve investments made by Member Countries; contribute to the harmonization of exchange rate, monetary and financial policies of Member Countries.

103. The FLAR is defined in its Constitutive Agreement as a juridical body of Public International Law with its own patrimony, confirmed by the Assembly, the Directory, and the Executive Presidency. Its associate countries are Bolivia, Colombia, Ecuador, Costa Rica, Peru, Uruguay, and Venezuela. Other countries of Latin America, such as the *Asociación Latinoamericana de Integración* (Latin American Integration Association (ALADI)) members, can join FLAR. Its headquarters are in Bogota D.C., Colombia.

104. The Andean Integration System is made up of two Social Agreements: the Simón Rodríguez and the Andean Health Organization Hipólito Unanue Agreement.

105. The Simón Rodríguez Agreement was signed in 1973 and subsequently amended in 1976. In that time, it was designed as an exclusive forum of Ministers of Labour of the Andean countries. The Governments of Bolivia, Colombia, Ecuador, Peru, and Venezuela signed the Simon Rodriguez Agreement, convinced of the need to strengthen policy coordination in the social and labour issue, which will be crucial in the progress of the Andean Common Market and the Subregional Social Agenda and in order to orient these social and labour issues within a framework of coordinated subregional action, while promoting also the active participation of the Andean business and labour sectors, to establish an institutional basis to effectively contribute to the development of social and labour issues under the Andean Integration System.

106. Its objectives are to:

(1) propose and discuss social and labour initiatives that would constitute an effective input for the implementation of the subregion's Social Agenda and contribute to the activities of the SAI bodies;
(2) define and coordinate Community policies for promoting employment, labour education and training, occupational health and safety, and labour migration, as well as any other matters the Member Countries may decide upon; and
(3) propose and design cooperation and coordination actions among the Member Countries with regard to Andean social and labour matters.

107. The Agreement was very dynamic during the 1970s, approving the Andean Instruments of Social Security and Labour Migrations through Decisions 113 and 116 respectively. It also carried out comparative studies of labour legislation and social security and issued a document on the Occupational Situation in the Andean Countries. However, in 1983, it stopped working. Nevertheless, there was a consensus on the need to bring this Agreement up to date 'in order to turn it into the qualified instrument that permits the accomplishment of the great social objectives proposed in the process of integration'.[13]

108. To that end, the Labour Ministers of the Member Countries of the Simon Rodríguez Socio-Labour Integration Agreement, in a meeting in Cartagena de Indias, Colombia on 20, 21, and 22 May 1999, issued the Declaration of Cartagena de Indias. The Declaration stated that it was essential that the Simón Rodríguez Agreement become the competent instrument to spur the social and labour process of integration of the Andean Community and serve as a foundation to prepare and design plans of action and strategies to improve the living and working conditions of the inhabitants of the subregion. They considered the Agreement to be indispensable and proposed that said instrument be brought up to date in order to serve as a tool to promote the participation of the social partners and achieve a productive transformation with justice and equity.

109. In this context, the Protocol of Substitution of the Simón Rodríguez Agreement was signed by the Foreign Ministers of the Member Countries of the Andean Community in the City of Valencia, Republic Bolivariana de Venezuela, on 23 June 2001, after more than two years of intensive work undertaken by the Advisory Council of Labour Ministers of the Andean Community in the formulation of the corresponding technical project.

110. As the name implies, this Protocol replaces the text of the original agreement signed in 1973, and its amendment of 1976. In the first instance, the Simón Rodríguez Agreement operated as an exclusive forum of Ministers of Labour of the Andean countries. The current Protocol of substitution of the Simón Rodríguez becomes the privileged space of convergence and coordination of interests of the three sectors involved in the social and labour issues in the Andean integration process that is the Advisory Council of Ministers of Labor, Andean Business Advisory Council, and Andean Labor Advisory Council. This new format of the Agreement as a tripartite forum for social and labour issues of the CAN became one of its most distinctive features and places, certainly at the forefront of similar spaces into other processes of integration in our continent.

111. The Protocol of Substitution of the Simón Rodríguez Agreement states that it would take effect when all of the Member Countries deposit their Instruments of Ratification with the Andean Community General Secretariat. Since all Member Countries of the Andean Community and Venezuela meanwhile, according to its laws, have deposited their instrument of ratification with the SGCAN, the Protocol of Substitution of the Simón Rodríguez Agreement entered into force.

112. Here are the chronological dates of deposit of the instrument of ratification of the Protocol of Substitution of the Simón Rodríguez Agreement:

Peru: 5 December 2001.

Ecuador: 14 April 2003.

13. Aparicio Valdez & Morgado Valenzuela, *Estudio sobre la Integración Sociolaboral Andina. En especial el Convenio Simón Rodríguez* (Lima, Peru, 1999).

Bolivia: 2 December 2004.

Venezuela: 2 May 2005.

Colombia: 12 June 2015 71e. The Protocol of Substitution of the Simón Rodríguez Agreement entered into force on 12 June 2015, being open to the adherence of any other country that becomes an Associate Member of the Andean Community, taking into account the procedures duly indicated by the Andean Council of Foreign Minister and the Commission of the Andean Community.

113. The Hipólito Unanue Agreement is a SAI institution created to coordinate and support the individual and collective efforts made by the Member Countries to improve people's health. The incorporation of the Hipólito Unanue Agreement into the CAN institutional structure was accomplished through Decision 445, approved by the Andean Council of Foreign Affairs Ministers on 10 August 1998. Its headquarters are in Lima, Perú.

114. The Executive Secretariat is the highest authority of the Andean Health Organization Hipolito Unanue Agreement. Its main function is to serve as facilitator of the mandates of the Health Ministers, issued at the meetings of ministers, held annually.

115. The Simón Bolívar Andean University is an institution devoted to research, teaching, post-university training, the provision of services, and promotion of a spirit of cooperation and coordination among the Subregion's universities. It is responsible for the elaboration and execution of teaching programmes that include theoretical as well as practical training. It carries out programmes of post-university formation primarily for professionals who are university graduates with qualified experience. It also prepares high-level scientific research and studies, especially on Natural Sciences, Social Sciences, Education, and Technological Sciences.

116. The university's headquarters are in Sucre, Bolivia. It has branches in Quito, Ecuador; La Paz, Bolivia; and offices in Bogotá, Colombia and Lima, Perú.

117. The Cartagena Agreement has opened the possibility of creating new bodies and institutions within the Andean subregional integration framework.

Chapter 3. The Results of the Process

118. The progress in the Andean integration process can be gauged by a group of indicators that allows us to establish the changes that have taken place within it. The following paragraphs deal with the advances that have been made in the regulatory framework and in community financing, as well as the changes in the enlarged market, foreign relations, physical integration, and in the development and integration of the borders.

§1. Advances in the Regulations Framework

119. The Andean Group has a long legislative experience. In a study carried out by ALADI in 1994,[14] it was found that the Andean Pact has the greatest range of legislations in effect in the Americas. Institutionally, the dynamics of the legislation is reinforced by the action of the Court of Justice of the Andean Community, in office since March 1996 and the Andean Parliament established in 1979, which also has a draft Additional Protocol to the Constitutional Treaty in 1997.

120. Between October 1969 and Mayo del 2011, the Andean Group adopted 717 Decisions and 1413 resolutions in order to enforce the established mechanisms in the Cartagena Agreement. The latter underwent many changes after the Protocols of Lima, Arequipa, Quito, Trujillo, Sucre, and Cochabamba.[15]

Between August 2011 and April 2015, fifty-one decisions were emitted – between 755 and 805 – regarding punctual themes referring mainly to tariff and commercial general policies, operative aspects of the statistic and information systems, encouragement of technology, agricultural application, and administrative precisions on the previous decisions. On the other hand, the validity of previous treaties and protocols was not altered.

121. The Andean legislation, in general, depends on the new trends in regional integration: an 'open regionalism' is practiced in the Andean subregion. There have

14. *See* the study for a programme of actions for the union and convergence among the different schemes of integration. Document prepared for the ALADI/CEPAL/SELA meeting of the government officials responsible for the commercial policy of Latin America and the Caribbean (Quito, Ecuador, 10–11 Oct. 1994).
15. The Protocols of Trujillo, Sucre y Cochabamba introduced modifications to the Cartagena Agreement.

been advances in community legislation, achieving more coherence and adjusting it in order to meet international trade challenges. The adopted Decisions have also made possible the basis for a healthy trade area free of competitive distortions.

122. Apart from Decisions related to the institutional and administrative areas, the Andean Community Commission has also issued laws on the free marketing of goods and has adopted the necessary Decisions for establishing a free trade zone; the regularization of technical measures, their accreditation, certification and metrology, as well as the establishment of regulations for safeguarding imports from non-Member Countries.[16]

123. Regulations have been adopted in order to avoid and correct practices that may disrupt stability within the subregion, such as restrictions on exports, restrictive practices on free competition, imports dumping, and subsidies of products from Member Countries of the Andean Community.

124. Special regulations for the qualification and certification of the source of the merchandise have been approved, as well as criteria and procedures for the setting of specific requirements for them. On customs matters, the Andean tariff nomenclature (NANDINA) was approved, as well as the Andean declaration on value, customs valuation, and international customs transit.

As it is known, the revision of the nomenclature is continuous, due to permanent changes in the technical processes and the emergence of new products. The most recent revisions of the nomenclature have been defined by Decisions 766 (25 November 2011), 794 (19 December 2013), and 789 (5 November 2014).

125. An External Common Tariff was adopted and has been introduced in the countries involved (Colombia, Ecuador, and Bolivia). The AFTA was fully set up and perfected on 1 January 2012, when the government of Peru completed the process of tariff reduction provided for in Decision 414 and completed its full incorporation into the AFTA in place since 1993 between Bolivia, Colombia, Ecuador, and Venezuela.

It means that the totality of the products that are original of the Andean Community will be able to circulate freely between the Member Countries without paying tariffs or burdens of any type.

The Politics regarding the commercial process are also a case of continuous modification. The tendency often results in slight changes, inside of a process aimed towards the aperture. The decisions in that regard are denominated as the Tariff Policies of the Andean Community. The latest have been Decisions 771 (7 December 2011), 801 (19 December 2014), and 805 (28 April 2015). Also important is Decision 770 (7 December 2011) regarding the Commerce facilitation in Customs matters.

126. Agricultural and Livestock Development. A system of agriculture, elementary safety, and environment conservation was created, as well as sanitary regulations for agriculture, technology, hygiene and sanitary inspection of cattle trade. In addition, there were programmes for the prevention, control, and eradication of fruit flies, foot-and-mouth disease, and cholera epidemics.

Some recent decisions refer to specific sectorial aspects. Such is the case of Decisions 774 (30 July 2012) referring to battle against illegal mining; 779 (11 March 2013) regarding an alert on phytosanitary matters for critics; 785 (11 March 2013) regarding the use of chemicals on agriculture (extended dues of restriction of applications);

---

16. *See* the Andean Community website: www.comunidadandina.org, Subregional Regulations.

793 (13 December 2013) about eradication of foot-and-mouth fever; and 804 (28 April 2015) about the registry and control of chemical insecticides of agricultural use.

127. Regulations for carrying out adaptation and efficiency tests on vegetables were approved, as well as quality controls on the seed trade and chemical pesticides for agriculture.

An Andean programme on rural development was established, which includes the Andean system of price range and a procedure for tariff preferences on products included in the Andean System of Tariffs.

These systems prevail and are in active periodic revision.

128. A strategy for the consolidation of the enlarged subregional market and the improvement of competition of the rice chain was adopted. The World Trade Organization (WTO) established guidelines for multilateral negotiations on agriculture, the harmonization of consolidated rights, and tariffs and coordination on matters of agricultural and livestock products among Member Countries. In 2011, work continued on the constitution of a sustained Subregional Forum, in an articulated set of instruments, were the Andean Network of Rural Development, the Observatory of Territorial Development, a Programme of Horizontal Cooperation, and an electronic Mechanism of communication and information. As far as the Nourishing Security, to put in execution the Project of Nourishing Security for the Indigenous Populations and the Regional Project of Nourishing Security.

Having achieved the objective of free commerce to the interior of the extended Andean market, the CAN now looks to perfect the communitarian norm that governs this market and its administration and to adopt measures that contribute to the transparency and eases the commercial process. In such a sense, actions are being carried out in the following fields: (1) improvement and administration of the extended market, (2) a political tariff, (3) norms of origin, (4) automotive agreement, (5) safeguards; (6) dumping and subsidies, (7) a Right corrective by differential tariffs, (8) free competition, (9) technical obstacles to commerce, (10) human health, (11) customs nomenclature, (12) customs valuation, (13) customs procedures and regimes, (14) farming products commerce and agricultural chains; and (15) an Andean system of farming health.

129. Trade services issues. A general framework of principles and regulations was adopted for their liberalization and the following regulations were approved:

(a) regulations for the international transport of merchandise and passengers on land routes;
(b) regulations that establish an Andean civil responsibility insurance;
(c) regulations for infractions, penalties for the international transportation on land, and weight and size limits for vehicles;
(d) regulations to promote air transport integration;
(e) rules to free access to cargo by maritime transport; and
(f) regulations establishing policies for the development of the merchant navy and multimodal transportation.

A decision on maritime guarantees and preventive embargo of vessels was also adopted. The objective was to cause the development and harmonization of the norm referring to the circulation of services to the interior of the Andean market; to contribute to the fortification of the capacities of the Member Countries for the advantage of the benefits of the intra-subregional commerce of services; and to support the preparation of the Andean countries with a view to the joint international negotiations in the matter of services, in special with the EU. In such sense, they are predicted actions for the: (1) fulfilment of Decision 659, identifying sectors of services object of deepening of the liberalization or normative harmonization, (2) tourism, (3) telecommunications and tics, (4) transport, (5) electrical interconnection, and (6) investments.

130. Decision 429 gave the ANDESAT Simon Bolivar Andean Multinational Enterprise the Community's first authorization to carry out an Andean satellite project and to utilize the Andean Community's orbit spectrum resource commercially. Therefore, with a view to dispose of an own system satellite, the Andean countries approved a set of community laws and developed actions to reach this objective. Now, the Member Countries are in a phase of political definition and normative for preservation, use and exploration definitive of the Orbital Spectrum Resource of the Member Countries of the Andean Community, in the sixty-seven position, through a definitive satellite.

Rounding 2015, the development of satellite technology was part of national politics on every country in the region. The Condor project, which proposes the integration of regional satellite, has been postponed, mainly due to the impulse generated by telecommunications.

131. With the purpose of eliminating the obstacles the free commerce in the sector, the Andean countries decided, in May of 1999, by means of Decision 462, the liberalization of the services of telecommunications, except those of sonorous broadcasting and television. For Regulations, the integration and liberalization of telecommunication services in the Andean Community for all communication services, except radio and television, were introduced on 1 January 2002. Regulation for the development of tourism within the Andean Community was also introduced. At the present time, the Andean citizens can only journey in the countries of the subregion identifying themselves with document official of identity, without necessities of passport and visas.

132. Foreign affairs. Guidelines on joint negotiations with third countries and other blocs were established. Guidelines for a Common Foreign Policy (CFP), a Community Policy for Border Integration and Development, and specific agreements with countries or groups of countries such as the United States (US) or the EU were adopted.

Mechanisms and procedures for the harmonization of policies and coordination of development plans of Member Countries were put in place. Regulations on financing and credit insurance on intra-subregional exports, matters of Information of Statistics, and financing and credit insurance to intra-subregional exports were also established.

The multilateral and binational agreements have had a great impulse in recent years, especially in the commercial-regulations ambit, which has widened its reach to intellectual-property areas, international arbitrary regulations, and even labour protection. In general, it can be mentioned that there is liberating impulse in Peru and Colombia, given the orientation of its latest governments, while in Bolivia and Ecuador, given equally for reasons of its economical politics, their orientation is more conservative.

133. Throughout the years, the Andean Community has striven to facilitate foreign investment. To achieve this purpose the following steps have been taken: an agreement to avoid double taxation among Member Countries; a special pact to negotiate agreements on double taxation among Member Countries and other States not belonging to the subregion; equal recognition of foreign capital, patents, trademarks, licenses, and royalties; and a uniform regulation for Andean multinational enterprises.

134. Common regulations were adopted for the protection of rights of the obtainers of vegetable varieties and on access to genetic resources, industrial property, intellectual rights, and other matters. Also, a decision was adopted for the protection and recuperation of the cultural, archaeological, historical, ethnological, paleontological, and artistic patrimony of the Andean Community.

The communitarian policy in the matter of intellectual property includes the regime of invention patents, models of utility, industrial schemes of layout of integrated circuits, designs, commercial marks, mottos, commercial names, labels, and geographic indications, regulated in Decisions 486 and 632; the rights of author and connected rights, regulated in Decision 351; rights of the regulated obtainers of vegetal varieties by means of Decision 345; and access to genetic resources established by means of Decision 391.

The negotiation of the Trans-Pacific Partnership (TPP) is symptomatic due to this alignment and the changes in the orientations of international treaties. The TPP tries to create an area of integration within the influential area of the Pacific, on the margins of China and Europe (while competing with APEC) with special emphasis on intellectual-property regulations, which has solely been supported, and with difficulty, by Peru.

135. The basis for a subregional technological policy was adopted, as well as a programme for cooperation in research and scientific and technological training within the Member Countries under the structure and functions of the Andean Council of Science and Technology.

It is important to mention, especially the progress made on the Decision 776 of 6 November 2012, on the thematic agenda of Andean science and technology.

136. On the liberalization of the movement of people within the subregion, an Andean system of Social Security, labour migration, and an Andean card of migration were approved. The national documents of identity were acknowledged and the Andean passport was created.

Decisions 501–505 of 2001 fulfilled this role in 2001. In 2003, by Decision 545, the Andean Instrument of Labour Migration is generated, and in 2004, by Decision 583, the Andean Instrument of the Social Security affirms. The Andean passport is effective but in addition national identification documents are used with the same aim in the countries of the area, and it was even extended towards the countries of the MERCOSUR (2009).

137. For the physical border integration, an Andean system of highways was adopted as well as a community integrating and border development policy and a regulation on Border Integration Zones (BIZ), and Binational Border Centre Assistance.

Bolivia is a special case, so collective measures have been adopted to support that country and an Andean joint plan was set up to aid in solving transportation and communication problems stemming from its land-locked location. The Andean Group is the most experienced group in solving disputes and controversies in the American Continent.

138. With these legislative actions, Andean integration has contributed to the process of promoting economic competitiveness in the Member Countries of the Andean Group, not only within the subregion but also with third countries. Steps have been taken to set up the Andean economic area and for its insertion in the world market.

§2. Community Financing

139. Financial cooperation in the Andean Community is carried out through the CAF[17] and the FLAR.[18]

I. The Andean Development Corporation

140. The Agreement of Cartagena established the political framework of the Andean subregional group and proposed the adoption of a joint model of economic, social, and commercial development between countries that presented/displayed similar characteristics and that they looked for to obtain the benefits that generally, in the scheme of regional integration of the time (ALALC), were reserved to the greatest nations.

Two years later, on 8 June 1970, CAF initiated its operations formally, fixing its seat to Caracas, Venezuela. It is possible to emphasize the importance of the futurist vision that had the editors of the Agreement, because this has allowed the Corporation to act with the flexibility necessary to adapt to the changes generated in the regional and worldwide surroundings and continuously to align its internal management with the growth of its businesses.

With the amendment of CAF's articles of agreement, other Latin American and Caribbean nations have been incorporated as members with the same right as the founding nations. Under this amendment to the agreement, which was executed in 2007, Argentina, Brazil, Panama, Paraguay, and Uruguay became Member.Countries.

141. During its forty-two years of activities, CAF has supported the integration process. It focused its activities on the process of integration and linked its operational policy to the 'Industrial Program', and to the 'Freedom of Market Program'. CAF offers financial products and services to the governments of the States' shareholders and to the public, deprived, and mixed organizations domiciled in the region.

142. During the 1980s, the emphasis was on national projects of production and development and the attraction of foreign capital outside the subregion. The 1990s show a movement of resources from industrialized countries to the region. CAF, acting as a link between the region and the international capital markets, finances the productive infrastructure development, especially the road transport and border integration process.

---

17. The Andean Development Corporation was constituted before the signing of the Cartagena Agreement on 7 Feb. 1968 and began its operations on 8 Jun. 1970. Bolivia, Ecuador, Colombia, Chile, Peru, and Venezuela took part in it. Chile withdrew from it in 1976.
18. The FLAR was created on 12 Mar. 1991.

It promotes the development, consolidation, and integration of financial and capital markets within the contributing countries, especially in the Andean Region, and fosters commerce, investments, and new business opportunities as well.

143. The present agenda of proposed development by CAF aims at the profit of a high growth, sharp, sustainable, and of quality. The profit of this objective requires the preservation of the advances reached in macroeconomic stability; improvements of the microeconomic efficiency; and a decided impulse to initiatives that promote a greater fairness and social inclusion and the reduction of the poverty in a context of environmental sustainability. These conditions are indispensable to face coherence and clarity, the challenges, and collective problems of the region. This integrated vision is a product of an important public diffusion and research programme of the knowledge in development subjects and policy that has been translated in a set of complementary activities to the financial management and of businesses of CAF, aligned with its strategic targets and directed to offer to support and institutional fortification to its shareholders.

144. CAF also supports the managerial sector, from large corporations to micro-enterprises, and backs the structural reform processes that are taking place within the shareholder countries. It is assisting them in the modernization of their economies and helping to increase their competitiveness in the global economy.[19]

145. During the past four decades, CAF has undergone a remarkable growth in its operations. The credits approved were over USD 499 million in 1970–1979, USD 2,052 million between 1980 and 1989, until it reached USD 20,463.7 million in the period 1990–1999. Since 2000–2010, these ciphers continue to rise while successfully introducing bond capitalization. Loans only for the period 2006–2010, exceeding all previously mobilized in the five years, have accumulated USD 39,798 million. In 2010, in approving disbursements USD 10,533 million, USD 5,796 million were sovereign capital and USD 4,737 million not sovereign capital.

146. Its loans to Member Countries were over USD 151.6 million in 1979, USD 416.7 million in 1989, and USD 4,615 million in 2000. The past decade has seen a ten-fold increase. Its assets have grown from USD 268.8 million in 1979 to USD 686.2 million in 1989 and USD 5,844 million in 2000. The net patrimony was USD 100.3 million in 1979, USD 408.3 million in 1989, and USD 1,629 million in 2000. The funds of the year 2010 have grown up to USD 13,878 million.

Towards 2015, the investments of the fund ascended to USD 18,955 million, of which 44.8% were investments in the Andean Community. It is important to note that during June 2014–2015, the Andean Community's participation on investments passed from 35.1% to 44.8%, making this fund a source of primordial importance for the region.

19. The Constitutive Agreement of the CAF (July 1999); CAF, *30 Years of Support to Integration and Sustainable Development* (CAF, August 2000) website: www.caf.com.

CAF. Loan Portfolio Distribution by Country (in USD Thousands)		
	As of 30 June	
	2014	2015
Bolivia	1,797,502	1,943,363
Colombia	1,983,464	1,549,177
Ecua dor	267,154	2,811,012
Pe ru	2,396,481	2,181,276
Andean Community total	**6,444,601**	**8,484,828**
Total (with adjustment)	**18,365,657**	**18,955,185**
Andean/Total %	**35.1**	**44.8**

Source: CAF (Proje cts).

147. The growth of the CAF has been made possible thanks to the leverage of the international capital markets and was achieved as a result of the degree of investment it has maintained since 1993 and which has improved enormously. In this sense, the CAF has become a financial institution of acknowledged prestige and international solvency, and it is the best Latin American issuer. Thus, in 2010, CAF had the award as the Best Multilateral Bank 2010, given for the famous magazine Latin Finance.

In 2015, CAF approved a project worth USD 80 million called 'Barrio Para MejorVivir' (Better Living Neighborhood) meant for Ecuador. In June of the same year, these projects could be found on the evolutionary phase on the Andean region: Double highway Santa Cruz-Warmes (USD 86.15 million), Water Program, Sanitation, Solid Residues, and Pluvial Sewage PROASED (acronym in Spanish) (USD 72 million), Greater Investments for irrigation MIRIEGO (USD 75 million) in Bolivia; Complementary Deed Live Route Phases I and II (USD 26,715 million), Program of Road Development Valley of the Chillos (USD 26 million) and Program Neighborhood for a better living II (USD 60 million) in Ecuador.

II. The Latin American Reserve Fund

148. The Latin American Reserve Fund (FLAR) is comprised of Bolivia, Ecuador, Colombia, Peru, and Venezuela. Its objectives are to provide balance of payments assistance to Member Countries by granting credits or guaranteeing loans to third parties; to assist in the harmonization of exchange, monetary and financial policies of countries and to help Member Countries fulfil their obligations within the framework of the Cartagena Agreement and the 1980 Treaty of Montevideo; and to improve investment conditions of international reserve funds carried out by Member Countries.[20]

149. The FLAR provides Member Countries with financial resources for their adoption of macroeconomic programmes of adjustment of structural problems in their balance of payments when there is a transitory lack of liquidity due, largely, to external problems.

20. Website of the FLAR: www.flar.net.

150. In addition, the FLAR has a mechanism in place to finance exports.

151. The credit modalities that have been mostly used by the Member Countries, throughout the history of the FLAR, have been credits and the granting of guarantees to support the balance of payments, liquidity credits, and exports financing.

152. The FLAR objectives are to assist with the financial requirements of Member Countries and offer opportunities for investment of the international reserves of Central Banks. It also manages its own investment portfolio.

153.

Latin American Reserve Fund				
	Subscripted Capital		Paid Capital (31 August 2015)	
Member Countries	Million USD	%	Millions USD	%
Bolivia	328.1	9	238.3	9
Colombia	656.3	18	476.7	18
Costa Rica	328.1	9	238.8	9
Ecuador	328.1	9	238.3	9
Paraguay	328.1	9	238.8	9
Peru	656.3	18	476.7	18
Uruguay	328.1	9	238.8	9
Venezuela	656.3	18	476.8	18
TOTAL	3609.4	100	2623.1	100
Prudential Reserves			262.3	

Source: FLAR.

FLAR has in 2015 limitations due to its capacity in capitals and competition with other financial organizations, but it also has access and greater regional compromise benefits. Rounding 2015, the annual movement was the order of USD 3,600 million to the Member Countries.

154. The FLAR has developed its own instruments for the managing of its active portfolio of international reserves. These investments have had larger returns than those obtained by other market alternatives in similar conditions of risk solvency and liquidity.

Besides, the FLAR offers the possibility of investing in instruments of high liquidity, security, and profit such as cash deposits or long-term deposits. It can also have the custody of securities and services of trusteeship.

§3. The Development of the Enlarged Market

155. The results of the study for the creation and consolidation of the Enlarged Market with respect to trade, investments, and intra-subregional tourism are being examined.

156. Following the trajectory worldwide, there has been vertiginous growth of the production of the Andean area. Thus, the regional product was of USD 28,574 million at the beginning of the process in 1970, but towards 1994, the number would have risen – in current terms – to USD 223 billion. In terms of constant dollars, in the year 2001, numbers were of USD 176 billion that increased to USD 461 billion in the 2010, after overcoming the end of the millennium crisis and the one of the 2008/2009. Rounding 2014, the size of the Andean region's product was USD 7,15,000 million with the exchange rate of 2010, and a growth of up to USD 7,55,000 million for 2016 was projected, probably greater compared to other world regions.

Andean Community PIB indicators 2013–2016

	2013	2014				2015	2016
Country / Region	Annual Growth	Annual Growth	MiLLU SD1010		P I B P.Cápita	Proy Crec	Proy Crec
Bolivia	6.8	5.4	34,139	10,562	3,232	4.4	4.4
Colombia	4.7	4.6	377,740	47,791	7,904	2.9	3.1
Ecuador	4.6	3.8	100,543	15,903	6,322	0.4	0.8
Peru	5.8	2.4	202,958	30,973	6,552	2.7	3.4
CAN	5.1	3.9	715,380	105,229	6,798	2.6	2.9

Sources: CEPAL and Population Division, NNUU.

According to CEPAL (Economic commission for Latin America, NNUU), and other international evaluations, the Andean Community's short and medium growth perspectives tend to decline regarding the successful 2003–2013 period, in which, excepting the effects of the international crisis perceived on 2009, a successful growth cycle was held, based on the exportation of commodities, specially metals, and petroleum derivatives.

The most favourable evolutions appear to be the ones of Bolivia and Peru, which are the countries that at the same time had the higher growths on previous periods. The diversification of exportations seems to be, in theory, the most important recommendation, along with the development of internal markets, especially insufficient, with the relative exception of Colombia. The exogenous factors that need to be overcome include the adversity of the lower global growth – especially from China – which has a growing influence on the Andean region – and the reflux of capitals due to the possible rise on the interest rate in the US and the response of other countries to this policy.

ANDEAN COMMUNITY: PIB BY ECONOMIC SECTORS

	2003	2004	2005	2006	2007	2008	2009	2010 p/	2011 p/	2012 p/
KIND OF ECONOMIC ACTIVITY										
ANNUAL RATES GROWTH										
PARITY OF SPENDING POWER (bases 2005)										
TOTAL PIB	3.7	5.6	5.4	6.5	6.6	5.9	1.6	5.5	6.4	5.3
Agriculture, hunting, forestry and fishing	3.7	2.2	4.3	4.1	3.4	2.1	0.4	0.9	4.9	2.5
Mines, quarries and hydrocarbons	2.8	8.5	5.3	2.8	0.5	8.5	4.7	4.9	8.1	2.7
Manufacture	4.5	6.9	5.5	6.8	7.9	4.5	-4.5	7.6	3.6	1.1
Provision of electricity, gas and water	4	2.5	4.1	4.8	5.8	4.3	1.4	3.5	4.1	6.4
Construction	4.3	8	7.5	11.3	9.4	11.1	7	7.3	4.2	12.5
Wholesale and retail	2.8	5.9	5.7	8.4	7.4	7.9	-1.4	8.3	6.7	5.2
Hotels and restaurants	5.6	6.9	4.9	6.8	7.7	6.9	3	6.2	7.7	7.1
Transports, storage and communications	4.5	6.4	7.7	9	11.4	7.2	2.1	4.9	7.7	5.9
Financial intermediation	4	4.5	8.3	12.6	12.1	9.8	4.6	4.9	13	13.4
Public administration and defense	2.6	4.7	4.6	4.8	4.9	3	6.2	4	5.4	4.9
Other services	3.1	4.3	4.3	4.5	5.1	4.6	2.5	3.8	5.5	5.1
Financial Intermediation Services. Indirectly measures	-9.9	-6.4	6.3	16.1	11.5	8.6	4.8	6.9	13.6	21.2
Net Taxes on products	5	5.9	6.5	8.8	9.3	6.9	-2.5	8.4	11	6.6

p/ Preliminary.

Survey: Estadísticas sobre Cuentas Nacionales Trimestrales (Decision 565) (Resolution 1052).

Elaboration: General Secretary of the Andean Community Statistics.

CAN's information indicates that the sectorial structure of the IBP, at the time of the first trimester of 2013, was commanded by the Other Services sector with 21.1%. This sector includes mainly real estate, entrepreneurial, and rent activities, as well as private homes with domestic service and extraterritorial organization, the first listing being the substantial part. It must be taken into account that under the denomination of entrepreneurial activities (of support to enterprises, to be exact), many enterprises that act as a nexus to the contracting are covered due to the outsourcing employment strategies and in reality occupy workers from different activities such as surveillance, transport, commercialization, tech services, and others. The second group is manufacture, followed by commerce and then public administration, mining and hydrocarbons, and construction (12.2%, 10.3%, 7.5%, 7.3% and 7.2%, respectively. These are followed by agriculture, farming, hunting, and fishing with 6.5% and the financial intermediation with 4.8%. Lastly, transport and storing, hotels and restaurants, electricity, gas, water, and communications have percentages of 3.7, 3.0, 2.8, and 2.3, completing the total PIB of 8.8% taxes to brute products.

A decrease in the primary sector is predicted for 2016, caused by already well-known international reasons and – for the agrarian case, especially in Ecuador and Peru – climatic effects given the presence of the El Niño phenomenon that began this year. If the seriousness of the situation was to be considered, the gravity of this happening would affect not only the Agricola sector on a direct manner, but also the concept of economy as a whole through its interrelations with agriculture and fishing and due to indirect effects such as spending in public prevention and mitigation of climate change.

157.

ANDEAN COMMUNITY. PIB BY SPENDING TYPE

	2003	2004	2005	2006	2007	2008	2009 p/	2010 p/	2011 p/	2012 p/
SPENDING TYPE										
ANNUAL RATES GROWTH										
% Parity of Spending power (It bases 2005)										
TOTAL PIB	3.7	5.6	5.4	6.5	6.6	5.9	1.6	5.5	6.4	5.3
Final Consumption	3	4.2	4.4	6	6.8	5.4	1.9	5.6	6	5
Private Consumption	3.2	3.9	4.1	6.1	7.1	5.6	0.9	5.7	6.2	4.3
Public Consumption	2.1	5.4	5.7	5.6	5.5	4	7.2	4.9	4.8	8.4
Gross Formation of Capital	4	8.1	12.7	18	15.1	17.8	-8.6	19.6	14	6.5
Gross Formation of Fixed capital	6.4	8.7	12.2	15.7	15.2	17.5	-3.6	13.1	13.8	9.5
Exports of Goods and Services	7.4	13.5	9.4	6	4.9	5.7	-3.8	3.9	9.7	5.1
Imports of Goods and Services	4.7	9.8	12.4	14.8	13.7	15.4	-10.5	18.8	15.4	5.6

p/ preliminary.

Survey: Estadísticas sobre Cuentas Nacionales Trimestrales (Decisión 565) y (Resolución 1052) Elaboration: General Secretary of the Andean Community.

Andean Community. PIB by Spending Type (Million USD in parity Spending Power – Base 2005)			
TOTAL PIB	874,152	906,766	3.7
Final Consumption	699,597	726,511	3.8
Private Consumption	582,087	603,060	3.6
Public Consumption	117,511	123,451	5.1
Gross formation of Capital	240,232	255,379	6.3
Exports of Goods and services	183,396	180,140	-1.8
Imports of Goods and services	249,073	255,263	2.5

p/ Preliminary.

Source: Estadísticas sobre Cuentas Nacionales Trimestrales Decision 565 y Resolución 1052.

Elaboration: General Secretary of Andean Community Statistics.

On the demand side point of view, the Andean Community structurally has an investment rate (forming of capital) that happens to be relatively low, with consumption dominated by the private sector disregarding the public, on a 5:1 ratio towards 2013. Regarding the commercial trade, the misbalance is manageable and will be discussed later on.

158. The modernization can, in addition, be appraised because the Andean growth of the present millennium occurs in a remarkably superior way in the investment before consumption. However, this capitalization is still sustained in imports and is not the result of the development of the industrial branches with a sufficient dynamics. It also denotes the deficiencies of redistributive mechanisms in the style of growth of these nations.

ANDEAN COMMUNITY. PAYMENT BALANCE RESUME. 2003–2012

Millions USD

TRANSACTIONS	2003	2004	2005	2006	2007	2008	2009	2010	2011	2012 p/
I. CURRENT ACCOUNT	-2,211	-992	370	2,980	-957	-8,416	-4,864	-13,451	-12,778	-16,750
1. TRADE BALANCE	1,621	5,056	8,248	12,319	10,945	6,901	9,415	8,420	16,013	13,438
Exports FOB	30,948	40,147	52,356	66,062	77,999	95,459	80,247	100,931	135,870	143,037
Imports CIF	-29,327	-35,091	-44,108	-53,743	-67,054	-88,558	-70,832	-92,511	-119,858	-129,599
2. SERVICE BALANCE	-3,270	-3,556	-4,260	-4,510	-5,571	-7,217	-5,638	-7,770	-8,727	-9,512
3. FACTORS RETURN	-7,323	-10,171	-12,717	-15,683	-18,735	-21,049	-20,076	-25,141	-32,097	-32,324
4. TRANSFERS	6,761	7,678	9,099	10,854	12,404	12,950	11,435	11,041	12,033	11,647
II. FINANCING CAPITAL ACCOUNT	1,767	5,656	2,771	1,272	17,425	16,869	9,083	16,846	23,372	39,136
III. ERRORS AND OMISIONS	812	360	579	-217	-245	-345	-1,539	808	-472	1,281
IV FINAL BALANCE (I+II+III)	368	5,024	3,720	4,035	16,223	8,109	2,680	4,203	10,122	23,667

p/ Preliminary.
FOB: Free on board.
Source: Central Banks of Member Countries.
Elaboration: General Secretary of the Andean Community.

To summarize, it is important to highlight that, towards 2015, the scenario is constantly changing in a preoccupying manner. After the boom in exportations due to the elevation of prime-matter price, the economic history seems to take a turn towards considerable decrease of these prices that was initiated in 2014. The economic observers seem to agree that the demand of these products will keep on decreasing, especially due to a minor growth from China and the slowness in the growth of the industrialized countries still affected by the financial crisis of 2008–2009. The very possible rise in interest rate by the US goes in the same direction – by bringing capital to its banks – by affirming a restrictive tendency on Latin American countries and, in this case, the Andean Community.

Nevertheless, disregarding the differences in policies, the Andean countries enjoy a relative macroeconomical health and consider that they will be able to resist the restrictions of demand until after the global growth is re-established along with its reserves – facing the possible crisis of their balance of payments – and the successive amplification of commercial bonds and the reconsideration of internal markets. It is considered that an assertive combination of commercial politics and the reinforcement of the macroeconomical foundations can make it possible for growth to re-establish and stay.

159. In spite of the positive balances of the trade balance, the commitments of the external debt and repatriations of capital in a scene are the reasons for the constant deficit of the balance in current account. The recent crises of capital have accelerated the exits of capitals but also the entrances, which allows a positive balance of the financing.

The Andean Community's balance of payments has been showing a negative income in the current account, which is negative and ascending, due mainly to the rent of factors, and in a lower impact to a negative balance of services. In both cases, this negative balance exists due to the impact of return of rents by foreign operations in the area.

Latin America and Andean Community. Payment Balance								
	Exports of goods FOB		Exports of services		Imports of goods FOB		Imports of services	
	2013	2014	2013	2014	2013	2014	2013	2014
Latin America	**1,116,348**	**1,083,027**	**152,301**	**154,015**	**1,104,135**	**1,091,421**	**231,033**	**228,835**
Andean Community	**140,485**	**135,385**	**15,806**	**16,387**	**134,865**	**139,692**	**25,658**	**27,091**
Bolivia	11,657	12,266	1,104	1,242	9,338	10,535	1,731	2,341
Colombia	60,281	56,982	6,859	6,937	57,101	61,676	12,788	13,523
Ecuador	25,686	26,604	2,029	2,334	26,178	26,672	3,524	3,553
Peru	42,861	39,533	5,814	5,874	42,248	40,809	7,615	7,674
	Balance of goods and services		Income balance		Balance of currents transfers		Current account balance	
	2013	2014	2013	2014	2013	2014	2013	2014
Latin America	**-64,396**	**-81,209**	**-155,091**	**-144,329**	**58,928**	**60,934**	**-160,559**	**-164,604**
Andean Community	**-4,233**	**-15,012**	**-28,109**	**-135,419**	**11,609**	**12,079**	**-20,734**	**-28,404**
Bolivia	1,692	632	-1,908	-1,707	1,270	1,084	1,054	10
Colombia	-2,749	-11,280	-14,175	-122,857	4,594	4,357	-12,330	-19,781
Ecuador	-1,988	-1,287	-1,395	-1,527	2,399	2,264	-984	-602
Peru	-1,188	-3,077	-10,631	-9,328	3,346	4,374	-8,474	-8,031

Source: Cepal. Economic Study of Latin America and the Caribbean 2015.

I. Trade

160. After reaching the goal of establishing a free trade zone among the countries of the Andean Community, it now seeks to improve the rules governing the market expanded to promote actions that contribute to transparency and facilitate the free flow of goods. As such activities are proposed in the following fields.

The improvement of the free trade area involves taking a series of measures to counter the barriers to the free movement of goods into the Andean market and, at the same time, contribute to transparency and trade facilitation. This is how systems have been developed as the Andean Integrated Tariff System (ARIAN) and the 'Export Alert', which extends the Notification Information System and Technical Regulations (SIRT), among others.

161. In the Lima Summit (July 2005), the Andean Presidents had given clear mandates for the definition and adoption of a Common Tariff Policy. On 1 August 2007, by Decision 669, the CAN Commission ordered the creation of a Group High-Level Working Tariff Policy Manager to recommend draft decisions for the establishment of a Tariff Policy of the Andean Community that incorporates all the Member Countries, not later than 31 January 2008.

162. Decision 416 adopted special rules for the qualification and certification of the origin of the universe of goods included in the NANDINA, applicable to trade in the expanded market of the Member Countries of Cartagena Agreement. For its part, Decision 417 establishes Criteria and Procedures for the establishment of Specific Requirements of Origin.

163. Member Countries have certain mechanisms to implement in their bilateral trade, corrections for tariff differences rights as set out in Decisions 370, 371, and 415 on the AEC, the Andean Price Band, and corrective measures for tariff differences between Peru and the other Member Countries. In carrying out the provisions of Chapter X of the Cartagena Agreement, Member Countries have, in the Decision 608, established the Standards for the Protection and Promotion of Free Competition in the Andean Community. It also has 456 and 457 Decisions to counter such practices of dumping and subsidies in the intra-Community trade, respectively, as well as Decision 283, in relation to practices in imports from third countries.

164. The Andean Community has a number of customs instruments that facilitate the commercial transactions of its members. Among them are the Nomenclature Nandina (Decision 653), Customs Valuation Standards (Decision 571), the Community Customs Transit (Decision 617), Cooperation and Mutual Assistance between Customs Administrations of the Member Countries of the Andean Community (Decision 478), the ARIAN (Decision 657), the Andean Customs Training Programme (Decision 573), and the Andean Customs Control Regime (Decision 574).

165. Progress has been made to overcome the problems in agricultural trade within the subregion, and is given the Andean Price Band and the Andean Agricultural Health System. In addition, there are proposals to improve the productivity of oil and coffee chains. As part of the administration of the Andean Agricultural Health System, subregional register was updated – the emergency regulations and the Andean Information System and Monitoring Plant and Animal Health – and has established a working group to work with international agencies in support of priority activities.

166. In terms of volumes of trade in goods, the 2000–2010 growth has also been explosive. Exports from the Andean Community to the rest of the world vary from USD 26,199 million to USD 98,003 million, while imports vary from UDS 25,417 million in 2000 to USD 97,411 million in 2010. The total trade varies then from USD 51,616 million to USD 195,414 million almost quadrupling in eleven years, despite the severe global crisis of 2008/2009. The tendency of growth in commerce continued up until 2014, but since then has been weakened by mainly exogenous effects. The community has suffered the impacts of financial crisis and most recently, the fall of the prices in raw material after the continuous-growth period they had since 2004. It is hard to prevent the extension and profundity of this commercial fall as well as the impacts over the growth dynamics.

In the same period (2000–2010), exports ranged from intra-Andean Community from USD 2,020 millions to USD 7,810 millions, and imports vary from 2,182 to 8,503 millions. Then trade in the Community developed from 4,202 millions to USD 16,313 millions. These changes are greater than the overall international trade itself. It has also increased trade within the Community a little more than the whole of his trade, but there are still wide margins for growth.

167. The result of the trade balance has been usually positive for the Andean Community with respect to the relation of its commerce with the rest of the world. In recent periods, the decrease in prices in the commodities tends to weaken the situation that generally is compensated with the reduction of importations and changing politics. Another important trait is that the intra-regional commerce – within the Andean community – is relatively lacking and descendent in proportions – from 10% in 2003 to 7.5% in 2012 – giving in to the rapid increment of global commerce.

168. Towards 2012, and even in the following years, the main commercial associate of the Andean Community was the US and consequently the NAFTA Treaty (which includes Mexico and Canada). To this group, the Andean Community exports 32.2% and imports 29.7% ; with the US, in particular, the percentages are 28.3 and 22.1 respectively. Followed in importance, the EU with 14% of exportations from the Andean community and 13% of importations; China with 8.5% and 16.3%; following, we have the Andean Community itself with 7.5% and 7.7%. The most important tendency has been, since then, the increase in China's participation, equally in importations and exportations in what today happens to be the second commercial partner.

Andean Community: Foreign Trade in Goods						
Andean Community: Evolution of FOB Exports by Country Member						
(millions of dollars)						
CATEGORY	2009	2010	2011	2012	2013	2014
WORLD	**77,681**	**98,003**	**134,111**	**140,903**	**136,864**	**128,356**
Bolivia	5,249	6,714	8,779	11,606	11,444	12,496
Colombia	32,784	39,552	56,915	59,165	58,526	54,706
Ecuador	13,539	17,251	22,292	23,724	24,966	25,707
Peru	26,109	34,486	46,125	46,408	41,928	35,477
INTRACOMMUNITARY	**5,775**	**7,810**	**9,207**	**10,361**	**9,858**	**9,724**
Bolivia	535	636	714	1,194	1,259	1,320
Colombia	2,116	3,063	3,373	3,677	3,393	3,210
Ecuador	1,586	2,127	2,770	3,066	2,819	2,545
Peru	1,538	1,984	2,350	2,424	2,387	2,649
EXTRACOMMUNITARY	**71,906**	**90,193**	**124,904**	**130,542**	**127,006**	**118,632**
Bolivia	4,714	6,078	8,065	10,412	10,185	11,176
Colombia	30,668	36,489	53,542	55,488	55,133	51,496
Ecuador	11,953	15,124	19,522	20,658	22,147	23,162
Peru	24,571	32,502	43,775	43,984	39,541	32,798

Andean Community: Evolution of Fob Imports by Country Member (millions of dollars)						
CATEGORY	2009	2010	2011	2012	2013	2014
WORLD	**74,969**	**97,412**	**126,136**	**136,685**	**141,615**	**146,919**
Bolivia	4,432	5,353	7,613	8,236	9,353	10,464
Colombia	32,898	40,638	54,675	58,644	59,498	64,060
Ecuador	15,127	20,056	24,285	25,153	27,026	27,507
Peru	22,512	31,320	39,563	44,652	45,738	44,888
INTRACOMMUNITARY	**6,377**	**8,503**	**9,994**	**10,455**	**10,551**	**10,410**
Bolivia	430	518	687	750	822	869
Colombia	1,563	1,890	2,257	2,261	2,300	2,675
Ecuador	2,102	2,932	3,187	3,112	3,356	3,165
Peru	2,282	3,163	3,863	4,332	4,073	3,701
EXTRACOMMUNITARY	**68,592**	**88,909**	**116,142**	**126,230**	**131,064**	**136,509**
Bolivia	4,002	4,835	6,926	7,486	8,531	9,595
Colombia	31,335	38,793	52,418	56,383	57,198	61,385
Ecuador	13,025	17,124	21,098	22,041	23,670	24,342
Peru	20,230	28,157	357,000	40,320	41,665	41,187

Andean Community: Trade Balance by Country Member (millions of dollars)						
CATEGORY	2009	2010	2011	2012	2013	2014
WORLD	**2,712**	**591**	**7,975**	**4,218**	**-4,751**	**-18,563**
Bolivia	817	1,361	1,166	3,370	2,091	2,032
Colombia	-114	-1,086	2,240	521	-972	-9,354
Ecuador	-1,588	-2,805	-1,993	-1,429	-2,060	-1,800
Peru	3,597	3,166	6,562	1,756	-3,810	-9,411
INTRACOMMUNITARY	**-602**	**-693**	**-787**	**-94**	**-693**	**-686**
Bolivia	105	118	27	444	437	451
Colombia	553	1,173	1,116	1,416	1,093	535
Ecuador	-516	-805	-417	-46	-537	-620
Peru	-744	-1,179	-1,513	-1,908	-1,686	-1,052
EXTRACOMMUNITARY	**3,314**	**1,284**	**8,762**	**4,312**	**-4,058**	**-17,877**
Bolivia	712	1,243	1,139	2,926	1,654	1,581
Colombia	-667	-2,304	1,124	-895	-2,065	-9,889
Ecuador	-1,072	-2,000	-1,576	-1,383	-1,523	-1,180
Peru	4,341	4,345	-313,225	3,664	-2,124	-8,389

Source. Bulletin of CAN. Foreign trade.

The deterioration in the commercial scale of the Andean Community is evident from 2014, according to statistic information coming from CAN, in current terms that evaluate the series, without altering previous tendencies. The major impacts, in terms of millions of dollars – which by 2014 was around USD 10,000 million and is expected to surpass this in 2015 – were between Colombia and Peru, more damaging to Peru in relative terms, since it has an economy of lower dimensions. Peru finds itself favoured by the lower prices on important fuels, but strongly affected by the decrease in metal prices, which explain two-thirds of its exportations. The decrease in the price of petroleum and its by-products, especially gas, affect mostly the rest of countries in the region, which also happens to have its exportations more diversified.

169. Now let us see the Outer Commerce of services. The exports of services of the Andean Community to the world during 2001–2010 were increased, with an accumulated annual average of 9.1% – from USD 4.725 million in the 2001 to USD

10.336 million in 2010. In 2010, the category of Trips contributes 53% of the total, followed by Transports with 24% of Participation and Communications with 4%, whereas the difference is attributed to other services.

Andean Community: Foreign Trade of Services According to Sector. 2003–2012 Millions USD										
CATEGORY	**2003**	**2004**	**2005**	**2006**	**2007**	**2008**	**2009**	**2010**	**2011**	**2012**
Exportations	**4,882**	**5,682**	**6,458**	**7,550**	**8,488**	**9,600**	**9,600**	**10,555**	**11,688**	**13,122**
1. Transportation	1,302	1,496	1,698	1,907	2,163	2,487	2,303	2,631	3,131	3,273
2. Travel	2,429	2,857	3,254	3,858	4,308	4,852	4,962	5,518	5,886	6,566
3. Communication	309	376	403	453	498	504	496	451	624	668
4. Other Services	841	952	1,103	1,332	1,519	1,758	1,839	1,955	2,047	2,614
Importations	**8,152**	**9,237**	**10,718**	**12,061**	**14,098**	**16,921**	**15,448**	**18,340**	**20,959**	**23,209**
1. Transportation	3,046	3,805	4,681	5,117	6,098	7,638	5,820	7,585	8,116	8,892
2. Travel	2,196	2,309	2,497	2,869	3,313	3,684	3,678	3,960	4,587	5,112
3. Communication	206	245	267	327	338	363	491	441	467	544
4. Other Services	2,704	2,878	3,273	3,748	4,350	5,237	5,460	6,354	7,790	8,660
Services Balance										
TOTAL	**–3,270**	**–3,556**	**–4,260**	**–4,510**	**–5,611**	**–7,321**	**–5,849**	**–7,785**	**–9,271**	**–10,087**
1. Transportation	1,744	–2,309	–2,983	–3,210	–3,935	–5,151	–3,517	–4,954	–4,985	–5,619
2. Travel	233	548	757	989	995	1,168	1,285	1,558	1,299	1,454
3. Communication	104	131	135	125	161	141	5	10	157	124
4. Other Services	–1,863	–1,926	–2,170	–2,416	–2,831	–3,479	–3,622	–4,399	–5,742	–6,046

Elaboration: General Secretary of the Andean Community Statistics.

The exportations of services are of lower order in the Andean Community. Their incidence is around a tenth of the goods exportation, and its evolution is negative. The sum and the composition of the service commerce denote a scarce relative development of the productive structure, but it should also be noted that the process of its evolution is positive.

170. The heaviest listings in the commerce services of the Andean Community are transportations – derivate from the commerce of goods – and travel, associated to tourism. In transportation, the incidence of minor exportations is pretty clear in its actual adverse orientation. To refer to travel, for a change, the balance is growing and positive and can be promptly converted into a production motor of greater force than the actual, given its high capabilities.

The situation that relatively presents itself as the most adverse is given in the different activities included in the generic rubric of 'Others', in which most importance has been found in payments equally coming from commerce as is with insurance and other entrepreneurial services, which affect – due to its greater commercial activity – principally Colombia. The rubrics with most technical incidence, as they could be connected with informatics and technology in general, still don't have sufficient significance, they are in the range of 1%–2 % of total commerce income, which should be growing as importations, specially, technology of telecommunications.

II. Investments

171.

Andean Community. Direct Foreign Investments. 2003–2012
Millions USD

SECTOR BY SECTOR AND COUNTRY	2003	2004	2005	2006	2007	2008	2009	2010	2011	2012
ECONOMIC SECTOR	4,494	5,837	13,812	10,975	15,687	19,880	14,561	16,311	23,343	30,155
Agriculture, cattle ranch, hunt, forestry and fish	58	81	35	174	96	62	80	76	155	124
Mines, quarries and hydrocarbons	1,411	2,531	4,121	4,667	4,880	6,631	6,799	6,353	8,827	9,042
Manufacture	455	312	5,542	1,379	2,117	2,031	924	1,088	1,141	2,299
Electricity, gas and water	75	110	–245	–117	–58	988	–601	295	423	988
Services	279	173	182	273	495	995	386	416	85	203
Constructions	6	117	163	191	267	952	269	430	483	280
Trade	301	327	375	591	904	1,183	708	346	2,396	1,684
Transports and communications	533	169	416	1,136	430	1,069	480	–677	1,684	1,850
Tourism	4	0	1	0	0	0	8	4	0	0
Finances	95	301	579	662	1,386	1,283	842	1,411	588	1,828
Adjusted 1/	1,278	1,717	2,643	2,019	5,170	4,686	4,666	6,568	7,560	11,856
ZONE	4,494	5,837	13,812	10,975	15,687	19,880	14,561	16,311	23,343	30,155
NAFTA	511	1,505	3,319	1,973	2,151	2,443	1,312	10	1,342	1,040
Canada	32	272	50	–108	70	210	159	293	589	290
Estados Unidos	453	1,216	1,779	2,001	1,766	1,483	1,163	51	595	655
México	27	16	1,490	80	315	750	–10	–334	159	95

COMUNIDAD ANDINA	12	58	46	94	151	201	51	431	97	259
Bolivia	0	0	0	1	0	78	–78	0	2	2
Colombia	–4	31	8	69	100	37	55	277	38	52
Ecuador	5	14	12	4	0	13	5	48	18	17
Peru	10	13	27	21	51	74	69	106	38	188
MERCOSUR	105	456	414	577	825	453	293	868	560	717
Países no Especificados Not specified countries	26	–31	29	166	133	730	352	119	748	3,177
Chile	18	–100	11	107	83	709	293	63	704	3,087
Venezuela	8	69	19	59	50	20	59	56	44	91
AMÉRICA CENTRAL	315	177	58	384	617	916	493	610	765	790
UNIÓN EUROPEA – 27	771	139	696	1,218	396	3,192	1,128	1,372	3,015	574
RESTO DE EUROPA	181	67	3,799	94	54	1,222	917	390	321	706
ASIA	90	41	–12	154	130	396	336	77	117	225
ANTILLAS	766	974	667	702	–177	280	402	103	–318	95
OTROS PAÍSES	–14	–123	4	25	1,062	71	72	26	135	338
Adjusted 1/	1,834	2,678	4,790	5,450	10,323	10,391	9,205	12,294	16,556	22,234

1/. Included: utilities investments, Colombia oil no distributed by countries and adjust payments balance. Survey: Central Bancks of Members Countries.

Elaboration: General Secretary of the Andean Community. Statistics.

Until 2012, the foreign investment had been growing impressively in the Andean region. Measured in USD (assuming the variations in the type of exchange in every country), they had multiplied, in a decade, almost seven times. Appreciating the investment according to its activity branch, the derivate of the mining and petroleum sectors could be highlighted, which is equal to the investment in every other sector, in a historically constant manner. Following in importance are the industry, the commerce, the transportation, and communications, which at the same time have its associations in part, once again, with the hydrocarbon and mining sector.

The importance is significant, in this chart of the fraction of total investment that can't be distributed by countries due to consorted international activities and big companies focusing on petroleum and mining exploitation.

Regarding the origin on the other investments, the importance acquired by Chile in the region must be highlighted, especially due to its investments in Peru that affect basically every economic sector. The origin of investments in the extractive sectors happens to be diversified, as it was mentioned, with relevance for the US, Europe, and, most recently, China.

172. The Andean Multinational Companies (Decision 292) are defined as those in which 60% of the share capital belongs at least to investors of two or more countries of the Andean Community. To these companies, national treatment in the matter of public purchases of goods and services is granted ; the right to freely convertible currency remission of the totality of the dividends that are distributed; the national treatment in tributary matter is granted; and the right to establish branches in other Member.Countries.

173. In June 2004, the Secretary Generals of the Andean Community (AC), Allan Wagner, and of the United Nations Conference on Trade and Development (UNCTAD), Rubens Ricupero, sent to Sao Paulo, Brazil, the Andean Strategy of Promotion of Investments, with the purpose of impelling them towards and from the Andean countries. The launching jointly happened with the representatives of the national organizations of Promotion of Investments of the five Andean countries.

174. On that occasion, the Secretary General of the Andean Community Allan Wagner explained that the Andean Strategy of Promotion of Investments is to fortify the national efforts and to establish a public-private subregional network to coordinate joint operations oriented to assure the contribution the foreign investment to the process of integration and the effective development of the Andean Subregion. The Secretary General of the CAN showed, in addition, that the Andean countries recognize the importance of creating a propitious atmosphere so that the investment flows and develops, as much originating from the outside as between the Andean countries, which implies a regional dimension of the promotion activities and protection of the investments. This project has been developed in a positive way, so that the investments in the region – since has been seen – have been increasing, having itself even improved successfully the national conditions in the scope of commercializing the global processes in March.

175. In the past ten years, the evolution of the flow of Foreign Direct Investment (FDI) in the Andean Community has been positive; the FDI reception has a rate annual average of 13%. In the decade, two defined sections appear clearly: with the levels of FDI between USD 4 billion and USD 6 billion in 2000–2004, and in 2005–2008, the FDI registered levels that oscillated between USD 11 billion and USD 20 billion in 2009, a strong fall in the FDI reception was registered, nevertheless this recovered in 2010, registering USD 14,985 million.

Latin America and Andean Community. Brute foreign investment (a) 2012–2014 (million USD)

	2012	2013	2014 (b)
Latin America	**131,631**	**158,449**	**135,429**
Andean Community	29,131	20,189	21,366
Bolivia	1,060	1,750	648
Colombia	15,646	8,547	12,155
Ecuador	585	731	774
Peru	11,840	9,161	7,789

(a) Deduce investment of residents in the exterior and include reinvestment of utilities.
(b) Preliminary outcome.
Source. CEPAL. Estu dio Económico de América Latina y el Caribe 2015.

Recent information given by CEPAL, referring to brute investment, just external, for the period of 2012–2014, shows that important drops are being produced on the flux of inverted capitals, as a result of the recent crisis scenarios, that possibly will mark a short-term stop.

176. These reductions affect primarily Peru and Bolivia. On the other hand, the results favour Ecuador and show an inflexion and recuperation for Colombia – which holds more than half the investments – and for Peru – which shows a sustained deterioration. The prospect of smaller investments could be confirmed in the short term, but according to the observers in the mid-term the recovery would occur and the positive flow could be recovered.

177. The remittance from the exterior saw an increase during 2003–2012 in a continuous manner. The vast majority of these covers the transferences in money from private entities, and its meaning is lessened due to exportations. On the other side, its significance with respect to the investments has produced a drastic change on its importance, probably due to the growing influence of the foreign investment by enterprises.

The recent remittances of workers taken into account by CEPAL have come to an end, due to the situation of crisis in the origin countries. The remarkable fact is that Colombia, which means 40% of the total remittance on the region, shall not diminish its importance or level in the transferences.

The remittances received off the work of emigrated workers has a special significance in the region, since the composition of emigration has been historically changing towards middle-to-low social populations and can be interpreted as an important cry for help socially.

Andean community: Received Remittances of the Outside. 2003–2012 Millions USD										
	2003	**2004**	**2005**	**2006**	**2007**	**2008**	**2009**	**2010**	**2011**	**2012**
Remittances	5,694	6,313	7,510	9,225	10,979	11,466	10,312	10,019	10,549	10,393
Remittances %, according to:										
Tcurrents transfers (%)	83.9	82.0	81.5	84.0	87.6	87.4	87.8	87.2	85.8	87.2
Exports (%)	18.9	16.0	14.6	14.2	14.3	12.2	13.1	10.1	7.9	7.4
Foreign investments (%)	126.7	108.2	54.4	84.0	70.0	57.7	70.8	61.4	45.2	34.5
Fuente: Central Banks of Member Countries.										

Elaboración: General Secretary of the Andean Community. Statistics.
Source: Central Banks of Member Countries.

Elaboration: General Secretary of the Andean Community Statistics.
CAN. Remittment of emigrated workers 2012–2014 (million USD)

	2012	2013	2014
Andean Community	10,319	10,410	10,360
Bolivia	1,094	1,182	1,164
Colombia	3,970	4,071	4.093
Ecuador	2,467	2,450	2,463
Peru	2,788	2,707	2,640

Source. CE PAL. Estudio Económico de América Latina y el Caribe 2015.

III. Tourism

178. The statistics of tourism has a particular relevance due to it being potentially greater in short and middle terms, as much as to improve the social balance situation and the balance of payments, as for their significance for productive diversification while facing the exhaustion of the economy's growth, when such is supported by prime matters primarily coming from the mining and petroleum sectors.

179. Between the years 2003 and 2012 stats, three countries doubled their international arrivals – Bolivia, Ecuador, and Colombia – while Peru does not follow this trend and grows in a slow and little-significant way. This situation must have changed with prosperity due to the important gastronomic boom that happened in the country.

180. The main regional contributors of the international arrivals to the Member Countries of the Andean Community were North America, the one of greater participation with 24%, the Andean Community and Europe, contributing 21% and 19% respectively. According to the way of transport used by the international arrivals to the Member countries, the preference has been to use the aerial route. In 2010, approximately 65% registered their arrival by this way of transport. One of the main reasons for this choice is the geography and extension of our countries, the aerial route being the fastest and effective way to arrive at our destinies.

Between 2003 and 2012, the derivate incomes of tourists were doubled, and the balance of income/expenditure generated by this sector improved by over five times. But these numbers could be slightly higher, given the Andean Community's attraction towards nature, historical monuments, and gastronomy.

ANDEAN COMMUNITY: TOURISM INDICATORS, 2003 – 2012

INDICATORS	2003	2004	2005	2006	2007	2008	2009	2010	2011 */	2012 p/
RECEIVER TOURISM a/ (arrivals, thousands)	**2,949**	**3,440**	**3,888**	**4,136**	**4,621**	**4,879**	**5,133**	**5,488**	**6,468**	**7,105**
Income generated by tourism receiver (USD millions)	2,453	2,879	3,255	3,849	4,308	4,851	4,962	5,252	5,885	6,566
EMISOR TOURISM (Departures, thousands)	**3,527**	**4,030**	**4,486**	**4,875**	**5,208**	**5,366**	**5,597**	**6,003**	**6,573**	**7,456**
Expenses generated by the issuer tourism (USD Millions)	2,199	2,307 8	2,489	2,812	3,313	3,683	3,678	3,955	4,586	5,112
BALANCE (INCOME EXPENSES) GENERATED BY TOURISM (USD)	**254**	**572**	**765**	**1,038**	**995**	**1,169**	**1,284**	**1,297**	**1,299**	**1,453**
BY MODE OF TRANSPORT (arrivals, thousands)	**2,949**	**3,440**	**3,888**	**4,136**	**4,621**	**4,879**	**5,133**	**5,418**	**6,468**	**7,105**
Air	1,841	2,173	2,515	2,629	2,978	3,178	3,375	3,496	3,808	4,136
Earth	1,027	1,174	1,272	1,398	1,509	1,553	1,593	1,755	1,920	2,169
Aquatic	14	19	17	22	30	38	48	44	62	74
Not specified C/	66	73	84	86	104	109	116	124	678	726
BY RESIDENCE COUNTRY c/										
(arrivals, thousands)	**2,949**	**3,440**	**3,888**	**4,136**	**4,621**	**4,879**	**5,133**	**5,418**	**6,469**	**7,105**
Europa	621	715	806	840	930	990	1,012	969	1,067	1,123
Otros América	1,283	1,547	1814	1,990	2,255	2,370	2,523	2,759	3,073	3,332
Asia	41	51	57	60	73	76	73	66	84	107
ANDEAN COMMUNITY	**756**	**889**	**929**	**922**	**998**	**1,008**	**1,044**	**1,058**	**1,083**	**1,264**
Bolivia	66	75	82	93	96	96	102	96	97	113
Colombia	250	228	238	245	278	289	260	316	394	504
Ecuador	141	208	204	218	236	228	242	276	268	291
Peru	300	379	406	366	387	395	440	369	324	355
Not specified C/	**66**	**73**	**84**	**86**	**104**	**109**	**116**	**124**	**678**	**726**
Others	**181**	**165**	**198**	**238**	**260**	**324**	**364**	**443**	**484**	**552**

*/ Break in the series in Colombia since 2011 includes Colombians living abroad.

p/ Preliminary.

a/ Bolivia and Ecuador by country of nationality. Peru by residence country.

b/ Figures are for the account of the Central Banks travel.

c/ Figures correspond foreigners, Colombia does not discriminate the country of residence of Colombians abroad incorporate.

d/ Figures correspond to nationals of Colombia and Peru living in other countries.

Source: Compendio de estadísticas de la Comunidad Andina, 2003–2012.

Elaboration: General Secretary of the Andean Community Statistics.

181. The international tourists are mostly American in the past decades, and the amplification of the happening of these arrivals is relatively slow. In the near future, it is expected that tourism towards the region will keep on extending, the principal problem being the need for hotel and vital infrastructure, specially towards zones that are not the national capitals.

182. The exits from the Andean countries have doubled during 2003–2012 and are probably still increasing, even though their rhythm is lower than the arrivals. The Andean countries classify its exits by associating them with proximity, to Chile and Argentina and the rest of the continent, the US, and Europe. An important part of this behaviour can be found on the immigration restrictions by the US and European countries and even Mexico. The issuance of an American visa, in recent periods, has been liberated, and regarding the European Community, an important aperture due to the liberation of the Schengen visa to Andean countries is expected in 2016.

§4. Foreign Affairs

I. Political Area

183. The extension of the External Relations of the Andean Community has occurred along with the deepening of the integration process, being today an instrument that reflects the diversity of the Andean agenda and that allows to the CAN and its Member Countries to have a more solid international projection.

The external relations of the Andean Community give priority to Latin American integration, and they extend towards Europe, China, Russia, and India through diverse mechanisms of dialogue and cooperation in subjects of interest common in social, environmental, political, and the economic areas.

184. The CFP is not conceived in isolation of other areas of action of Andean integration; on the contrary, the CFP nourishes itself of the actions that in other spheres of integration are developed.

185. The Agreement of Cartagena establishes that the objectives of integration aim is, among others, to facilitate the inclusion of the Member Countries in international economic context, with a view to the gradual formation of a Latin American common market. In 1979, the Mandate of Cartagena defined the constituent instrument of the Outer Cabinet of Relations of the Andean Group, whose first attribution was to formulate the joint Foreign policy. In 1980, the Presidents signed in Riobamba, Ecuador, the Letter of Conduct that established the democratic character that must govern the subregional political ordering, as well as its commitment with respect to the Human rights, such as fundamental norm of internal conduct of the Member Countries.

186. The Protocol of Trujillo of 1996 incorporates totally to the Outer Cabinet of Relations in the legal ordering of the Andean Community, granting the faculty to him to make Decisions of binding character and reaffirming the mandate to formulate the foreign policy of the Member Countries in subregional subjects.

187. Protocol of Sucre of 1997 introduces in Agreement of Cartagena chapter specifically on Relations External, in that one needs that 'the Andean Council of Outer Ministers of Relations will formulate the CFP, for the subjects that are of subregional interest', by means, among others, of the agreement of joint political positions, the definition of a strategy directed to the deepening of integration with other regional and extra-regional blocks, the coordination of joint negotiations and the communitarian participation in international economic and commercial forums. Also, the Protocol incorporates a chapter on Associated Members, in which the conditions are defined to acquire this character.

188. Decision 458 established in 1998 the 'Common Foreign Policy Guidelines', defining its principles, objectives, criteria, mechanisms, modalities, and areas of action.

II. Economic-Commercial Fields

189. Fields of economic cooperation, trade and technical, have been important changes in recent years, especially due to the growing presence of emerging markets that were added to traditional intra-community, with North America and Europe fostering this diversification – also the presence of new blocks in the Latin American region, as well as, the relative independence and particularity of relations with some countries such as Chile and Mexico.

A. Latin America and the Caribbean

190. A key objective of the Andean Community is to contribute to Latin American integration through a comprehensive dialogue with other countries and integration initiatives in the region.

191. In South America, Chile, and MERCOSUR: Argentina, Brazil, Paraguay, and Uruguay, partner countries of the Andean Community. In these countries there is a relationship based on an important trade and the existence of common interests in social and political. Mexico and Panama have an active dialogue and a shared interest in increasing trade and political cooperation.

192. In these relations that integrate Latin America, it is important to mention that the Community of Latin American and Caribbean States (CELAC in Spanish) created on 23 February 2010, has a mechanism of integration, cooperation, and concentration of regional politics, comprised of thirty-three States of Central America, the Caribbean and South America: Antigua and Barbuda, Argentina, Bahamas, Barbados, Belize, Bolivia, Brazil, Chile, Colombia, Costa Rica, Cuba, The Dominican Republic, Ecuador, El Salvador, Grenade, Guatemala, Guyana, Haiti, Honduras, Jamaica, Mexico, Nicaragua, Panama, Paraguay, Peru, Dominica, San Kitts and Nevis, San Vicente and the Grenadines, Santa Lucia, Suriname, Trinidad and Tobago, Uruguay, and Venezuela.

193. The goal of this institution, with rules over the base of the historic legacy of the Rio group and CALC, is to promote regional integration, while also promoting political concentration, pushing the Latin American and Caribbean agenda in global summits, and to strengthen cooperation. Its relationships with the Andean community are still located at the margin of normal commercial treaties.

B. Republic of Chile

194. In 1969, Chile signed the Cartagena Agreement, however, seven years after in 1976, left it for dissent in trade barriers that contradicted its position of openness.

195. In 2004, Chile participated as observer in the XVth Andean Presidential Council. In 2006, through Decision 645 adopted on 20 September, Chile became an Associate Member of the CAN, thirty years after its exit. It signed on 24 November, the Act of Constitution of the CAN-Chile Joint Commission and held its first meeting.

196. Decision 666 of 8 June 2007 establishes the terms of the participation of Chile in the organs, mechanisms, and measures of the Andean Integration System and specifies the instances in which Chile will be invited to participate with voice. The second meeting of the CAN-Chile Joint Commission was held in Bogota in the year 2008. In furtherance of Decision 666 of 2007, Chile has participated actively in the following meetings and instances of the Andean Community.

197. In meetings. In the Andean Council of Ministers of Social Development, held in Lima on 18 August 2008. The Andean Migration Forum held in Quito on 4 and 5 September 2008. At the Seventh Executive Committee of the Andean Cooperation Plan for the Fight against Illicit Drugs and Related Crimes, held in Quito in November 2008. At the Seminar on Macroeconomic Convergence and Expert Meetings made in the first half of 2008. In the First Mesa Andean Civil Society Participation for the Defence of Consumer Rights on 12 August 2009, which Chile hosted. During the Second Andean Forum on Migration, held in Lima on 26 and 27 October 2009.

198. In instances. Chile participates in the Andean Health Organism – Hipólito Unanue. Amazon Andean Programme Environmental Education and Communication (PANACEA). Project to Support the Andean Community in the area of synthetic drugs (DROSICAN). Andean Executive Committee of the Plan to Fight Corruption. Andean Regional Conference on Employment.

C. MERCOSUR

199. The convergence objective-oriented relations between the systems integration of the Andean Community and MERCOSUR, to strengthen South American regional integration in both the commercial and the political dialogue and consultation. The most significant step was established by Decision 732, 2010, in which the Andean Community confirms the interest in promoting active participation of Argentina, Brazil, Paraguay, and Uruguay, in different instances of the CAN, in its capacity partners and encourages the creation of a Joint Commission to identify areas and mechanisms of such participation.

200. Previously, in 1998, the signing of a Framework Agreement was made for the creation of a Free Trade Area between the Andean Community and MERCOSUR, which lays the groundwork for the formation of this extended space and provides that the negotiations take place in two stages: first to negotiate a fixed tariff preferences and second to establish a Free Trade Agreement.

201. In 1999, the form of bargaining block by block (4+4) is replaced by the CAN negotiations with each of the States' Parties of MERCOSUR (4+1), while maintaining the ultimate goal. As a result, Colombia, Ecuador, Peru, and Venezuela signed with Brazil this year a Fixed Tariff Preferences Agreement as a first step to creating a Free Trade Area between the Andean Community and MERCOSUR. In 2000, the Member Countries of the Andean Community and Argentina signed a partial-scope agreement of economic complementation, which t effect on 1 August 2000.

202. In 2001, the Foreign Ministers of the countries of the Andean Community, MERCOSUR, and Chile in La Paz established a Mechanism for Dialogue and Politic directed to facilitate the conclusion of joint actions in the areas of political, economic, and physical infrastructure integration, relationships, external exchange of information, and social and cultural aspects.

203. In 2004, agreements on Economic Complementation No. 36 between Bolivia and the MERCOSUR Member Countries (signed in 1996) and the Economic Complementation No. 58 between Peru and the MERCOSUR Member Countries (signed in 2003) added the Agreement Economic Complementation No. 59, by which Colombia, Ecuador, and Venezuela, Member Countries of the ACN and MERCOSUR Member States, decided to form a free trade area through the expansion and diversification of trade and the elimination of tariff and non-tariff barriers that affect reciprocal trade.

204. Finally, before reaching Decision 732, Andean Council of Foreign Ministers, meeting in enlarged session with the Commission, adopted in 2005 Decision 613 by which it granted Associate Member status of States Parties to the MERCOSUR and defined the terms of its participation in the Andean Community.

D. United Mexican States

205. Mexico participated, in 2004, in the XVth Andean Presidential Council time, that in which the Heads of Member Countries agreed to encourage the establishment of a mechanism of political dialogue and cooperation with Mexico, and in 2005 participated as an observer in the XVIth Andean Presidential Council.

206. Mexico and the Andean Community signed the 2006 Agreement for the Establishment of a Mechanism of Political Dialogue and Cooperation, by which the parties undertake to advance cooperation in areas such as facilitation of movement of persons, consular cooperation, disaster prevention, and climate change, among others.

207. In 2007, the First Meeting of the Mechanism of Political Dialogue and Cooperation was held, which agrees on Political Dialogue and Cooperation on the following topics: dialogue on issues of common interest of the international agenda, facilitating the movement of people and consular cooperation, prevention and management of natural disasters, and environmental protection and climate change, among others.

E. UNASUR

208. Noteworthy in the South American region is the new presence of the Union of South American Nations (UNASUR), which contains CAN countries. The UNASUR aims to build a South American identity and citizenship, as well as to develop an integrated regional space. This new model of integration will include all the progress achieved so far by the processes of MERCOSUR and the Andean Community, as well as the experience of Chile, Guyana, and Suriname. The ultimate goal is to, and will, stimulate a more equitable, harmonious, and integral part of South America.

209. Most Member Countries have ratified the Treaty, which entered into force almost three years after its signing, held in Brasilia on 23 May 2008.

F. European Union

210. The Andean Community and its Member Countries have long-standing relationships with EU and its Member States, which are based on historical ties, interests, and shared values. In recent decades, the bi-regional links have been strengthened not only in trade but also in politics and cooperation as well. Witness to this are the signing of a cooperation agreement 'third generation' in 1992, the establishment of Specialized Dialogue on Drugs in 1995, the political dialogue in 1996, the signing of the Agreement on Political Dialogue and Cooperation in 2003, and the increasingly significant trade and investment flows between both regions.

211. The European Community and the Andean Pact signed in 1993 a Cooperation Agreement that was implemented in 1998. In 1996, the European Community and the Andean Pact signed in Rome a Statement of Joint Policy Dialogue, thus providing an institutional framework for dialogue, hitherto held informally. This Declaration, which would hold dialogue through meetings of high level, would revolve around issues of bi-regional and international common interest.

212. In 2003, the Agreement on Political Dialogue and Cooperation Agreement between CAN and the EU was signed. This Agreement had been ratified by the Andean region and was expected to prompt ratification by all European states. Finally, in 2004, by Decision 595, the Andean Council of Foreign Ministers adopted the Agreement on Political Dialogue and Cooperation.

213. At the Fourth Summit EU – LAC in 1996, the Heads of State of the Andean Community and EU took the decision to initiate a process leading to the negotiation of an Association Agreement with three pillars: political dialogue, cooperation, and an agreement on commercial use.

214. Decision 667 defines the general framework for the negotiations of the Association Agreement between the Andean Community and the EU. In this context, between 2007 and 2008 three rounds of negotiations were held to move towards an Association Agreement with three pillars: political, cooperation, and trade. The agreement includes a 'flexible' format that leaves each CAN Member Country the possibility of entering into the negotiation of different subjects at different rates and terms, so that from the fourth round they can perform at bilateral level.

G. Republic of India

215. The Andean Community and India set, in 1993, A Mechanism of Political Dialogue and Cooperation for the purpose of promoting the strengthening and diversification of their friendship, understanding, and cooperation, as well as the development of trade relations, investment, and cultural and scientific exchange.

216. The Mechanism of Political Dialogue and Cooperation aims to: (i) deepen mutual understanding between the parties; (ii) develop political dialogue and cooperation on issues of mutual interest; (iii) promote the expansion and diversification of trade and investment, and the study of mechanisms to facilitate access to their markets; (iv) promote science and technology; and (v) promote cultural exchange, and tourism.

H. Republic of China

217. In the year 2000. CAN and China signed the Agreement for the Establishment of a Mechanism for Political Consultation and Cooperation with the objective of strengthening the bonds of cooperation and trade, business and technology, and dialogue in international multilateral fields. That same year they performed, at the General Secretarial Headquarters in Lima, the seminar 'Business Opportunities between the Andean Community and the Republic of China' to also strengthen ties with the private sector in that country. In 2002 there was a shorter Ministerial Meeting and in 2004 another Second Meeting of Consultation, at vice chancellors level.

I. Russian Federation

218. The Andean Community and the Russian Federation, in 2001, signed the *Protocol for the Establishment of a Mechanism for Political Dialogue and Cooperation,* aimed at strengthening and expanding its relations of friendship, mutual understanding, economic cooperation, and scientific-technical and cultural ties. In 2004, they performed the First Meeting of the Mechanism of Political Dialogue and Cooperation where CAN expressed its interest in developing ties with the Russian Federation in fields such as combating terrorism, the global problem of drugs, illicit trafficking of small arms and light weapons, corruption, environmental protection, and the prevention and management of natural disasters. In 2008, there was a CAN consultation – Russia in Bogota trade.

§5. Physical Integration

I. Roads Infrastructure and Transports

219. Inasmuch as the transportation infrastructure for the integration process is being planned and programmed on a South American scale, the Andean Community countries are giving priority to the actions and projects provided for in the framework of the South American Regional Infrastructure Integration Initiative (SARII). At the same time, efforts are being made to reactivate the Andean Committee on Road Infrastructure (ACRI).

220. The ACRI is a forum for road infrastructure authorities from the Andean Community Member Countries that was established by Decision 271 in October 1990, for coordinating the execution of programmes, projects, and actions having to do with the Andean Road System. Today, the countries are coordinating the committee's reactivation.

221. The SARII Initiative is an institutional mechanism for the coordination of intergovernmental actions performed by the twelve South American countries. Its main purpose is to create a common agenda related to actions and projects of infrastructure integration regarding transportation, energy, and communications.

222. The SARII Initiative came up from the First Meeting of Presidents of South America held in Brasilia in August 2000, where the regional leaders agreed to take joint actions to promote the process of political, social, and economic integration of South America, including the modernization of the regional infrastructure and specific actions to stimulate the integration and development of isolated subregions.

223. In compliance with the mandate conferred at the First Meeting of South American Presidents held in Brasilia on 2000, the Ministers of Transport, Energy, and Telecommunications of the twelve countries prepared an Action Plan for the Integration of Regional Infrastructure in South America.

224. The activities developed in SARII are based on a geo-economic vision of territorial integration and the key role played by infrastructure, logistics, and the regulatory and institutional aspects, which more often than not prevent countries from making an adequate use of infrastructure.

225. The strategic objectives of SARII for 2006–2010 are focused on four action areas: (i) ensure the Implementation of the projects of the Agenda based on Consensus; (ii) work towards making a qualitative leap in the territorial planning process and the decision-making process related to investments in South American integration infrastructure; (iii) capitalize the Initiative's actions and experience gained in integration of zonal processes to support integration infrastructure-specific projects; and (iv) strengthen the outreach strategy of the Initiative.

226. International road transport in the Andean Community is regulated by Decisions 398 (passengers) and 399 (goods), whose purpose is to guarantee the efficiency of the service by spelling out the contractual conditions and the responsibility of both transporters and users in clear and precise terms.

227. In the area of ocean transport, the adoption of Decision 288 made it possible to eliminate reserved cargo at the Andean-level, thereby reducing freight costs significantly and increasing the hold capacity available for trade in goods.

228. The Andean Community Member Countries apply Decision 582 to the provision of scheduled and non-scheduled international air passenger and mail transport services, both separated and combined, among their respective territories and between these and third countries.

229. Community provisions adopted pursuant to Decisions 331 and 393 regulate multimodal transport operations in the subregion. These provisions create the appropriate legal conditions for promoting and boosting the supply and provision of multimodal transport services. Furthermore, the Regulations for the Registry of Multimodal Transport Operators were approved through Resolution 425 of the Board of the Cartagena Agreement.

The SARII´s (IIRSA in Spanish) agenda has been developing in a continuous matter, and it affects countries in the Andean area continuously. In August 2015, in Montevideo, the projects of different geographical areas were revised, of which, affected are some Andean community countries: The Andean axis, which includes the four members of the Andean Community and Venezuela, the Central Inter-oceanic and Peru-Brazil Bolivia; the Capricorn axis (includes Bolivia, Argentina, Brazil, Chile, and Paraguay); and the Amazonas axis (Peru, Ecuador, Colombia, and Brazil). In this event, the level and phase of the projects were informed: 114 projects making roughly USD 30.973,6 million (17%), 186 projects in pre-execution USD 56.134,8 million (30.8%), 178 projects in execution USD 69.214,5 million (37.9%) and 115 concluded projects USD 26.112,7 million (14.3%)

II. Telecommunications

230. The major strides taken in microelectronics and computer science laid the groundwork for the revolution in telecommunications during the last three decades of the twentieth century. Today the entire world is interlinked, thanks to telecommunications satellites, fibre optics, television, radio, and telephony.

231. In this context, the telecommunications sector in the Andean Subregion has grown heavily and undergone numerous changes. State monopolies have been privatized and the markets have been opened to competition while, at the same time, supervisory institutions were being created.

232. The changes in the telecommunications market have also demanded regulatory changes in order to ensure good market operation. Within the sphere of operation of the Andean Community, the advances are grounded in Presidential Guidelines and Mandates and in a broad body of legislation that reinforces the development of the Andean telecommunications sector.

233. In order to remove the obstacles to free trade in the sector, the Andean countries agreed in May 1999, through Decision 462, to liberalize all telecommunications services, except for sound broadcasting and television. The Andean countries also approved a series of Community legal provisions and took action to obtain a satellite system of their own.

234. The CAN Member Countries registered orbital positions within the orbital arc of 60 o–70 o with the International Telecommunication Union (ITU), giving them the right to commercially exploit those positions.

235. With the adoption of Decision 395, they approved the Regulatory Framework for the commercial use of the Member Countries' Orbit Spectrum Resource (OSR), through the establishment, operation, and exploitation of Satellite Systems by private enterprises.

236. The Member Countries are at present defining the policy and regulations for safeguarding, using, and permanently exploiting the Andean Community Member Countries' OSR at orbital position 67°O, through a permanent satellite.

237. In November 1991, the Andean Committee of Telecommunications Authorities (ACTA) was created by Resolution No. VI. 144, with a membership consisting of representatives of the agencies responsible for regulating and administering telecommunications policy in each of the Member Countries. Its function is, among other things, to give the bodies of the Andean Integration System advisory assistance on telecommunications.

During recent periods, the telecommunication network has advanced rapidly through the introduction and development of satellites. With the purpose of having a satellite system for the Andean community, the Andean countries have approved communal norms and developed actions that aim for the realization of this objective.

In November 2006, the regulatory frame for commercial utilization of the OSR was approved on the Member Countries and the procedures to give communitarian authorization (Decision 654). Afterwards, in December 2008, the communitarian norm was adopted (Decision 707) for the Andean registry for authorization of satellites with coverage over the territory of the Member Countries of the Andean community.

In November 2009, the commission of the Andean community approved Decision 725, by which it gave the company New Skies Satellites B.B. communitarian authorization for the commercial utilization of the OSR of the Member Countries in the Andean community; all while being subscripted to a contract, which was concerted in February 2010.

Towards mid-2015, there were fifty registered satellites in the Andean community through twelve operating companies.

III. Integration Energetic

238. The First Meeting of the Council of Andean Community Ministers of Energy, Electricity, Hydrocarbons, and Mines, held in Quito in January 2004, defined the bases for the Andean Energy Alliance (AEA), to be established through efforts in five areas:

(1) construction of energy (electricity and gas) markets integrated through harmonized physical systems and regulatory frameworks;
(2) positioning in international hydrocarbon markets in a strategic context of energy security;
(3) promotion in the Andean countries of entrepreneurial development of 'energy clusters';
(4) framework for the negotiation and classification of energy services in the WTO and other international organizations; and
(5) development of the renewable energy sources theme and its tie-in with the environmental theme and with the PIDS.

239. Electric interconnection. Decision 536 'General framework for subregional interconnection of electric power systems and intra-Community exchange of electricity', approved in December 2002, gave the Community a legal framework for promoting the development of the electricity theme among the Member Countries.

240. As a result of this Decision, the Andean Committee of Electric Service Policy-Setting and Regulatory Agencies (CANREL) set to work with its Technical Groups: (i) Working Group of Electric Service Regulatory Agencies (GTOR), formed in June 2003, to formulate proposals for advancing the harmonization of regulatory frameworks needed for full subregional interconnection of electric power systems and intra-Community exchange of electricity; and (ii) Working Group of Electric Service Policy-Setting Agencies (GOPLAN), created in January 2004 to draw up proposals, coordinate efforts with Andean energy and electric power institutions, and reach agreements for fulfilling aspects of information access and coordinated project planning, with a view to the region's integration.

The Member Countries of the Andean community reaffirm their objective of having a general margin for the subregional interconnection of electrical systems, in which principles and general rules are established in order to create intercommunitarian exchanges within the Andean countries. This means to give in to a process based in the existent regulatory margin, the dispositions of national legislation viable in Andean countries, as well as the adaptation of facilitation for interconnections of electric systems of every country.

241. The electric systems of Colombia and Ecuador were interconnected in March 2003 pursuant to this Decision, and they produced important benefits for both Member Countries.

242. With the interconnection and full operation of the electric systems of Colombia and Ecuador, the interconnection of Colombian and Venezuelan electric lines, and the forthcoming electric interconnection of Peru and Ecuador – all as a result of Decision 536 'General Framework for subregional interconnection of electric power systems and intra-Community exchange of electricity' –, the Andean electricity market has reached its first level of integration. It should be added here that Bolivia announced in July 2005 that it had decided to adhere to that Community Decision.

243. Gas interconnection. The Action Plan of the Andean Council of Ministers of Energy, Electricity, Hydrocarbons, and Mines gave special priority to develop the gas theme in the Subregion. The Chairman of that Council of Ministers, in coordination with the SGCAN, accordingly called the First Meeting of the Ad hoc Group for Gas Matters, which took place in Lima on 13 and 14 November 2003. International organizations directly concerned with gas, such as Latin American Energy Organization (OLADE), Electronic Commission for Latin America and the Caribbean ECLAC, Inter-American Development Bank IDB and CAF, took special part in that meeting.

244. As a result of the meeting, it was decided to advance the execution of a working plan drawn from the document especially prepared by ECLAC for the meeting, which contains the following recommendations:

(a) With binational integration processes as a starting point, move ahead with criteria that are not only economic but also have a strong social component and that are aimed at long-term integral development. It is advisable to gradually build up an infrastructure system that will progressively improve the people's quality of life and contribute to that development. Therefore, these strategies should emphasize mechanisms that facilitate the access of poor sectors to clean and efficient energy sources, such as gas and electricity, in that way coinciding with the basic principles of sustainable development.
(b) Respect the natural role of regional international organizations with broad experience on the subject by reinforcing that role.
(c) Work on the orderly definition of an agenda of tentative efforts to induce the Member Countries to participate creatively in coordinating this long-term vision and its key objectives.

245. It was agreed at the First Meeting of the Council of Andean Community Ministers of Energy, Electricity, Hydrocarbons, and Mines to create the Permanent Group of National Experts on Gas, whose main responsibilities are as follows:

(a) Conduct studies of the potential demand for gas up to the year 2030, with realistic hypotheses and contrasting scenarios. Integral methodologies would be employed to consider demand within each country by regions and by homogeneous consumption or user groups, in order to determine foreseeable penetrations and the relative price conditions that would tend to ensure forecast fulfilment. Emphasis would be placed on the access of the poor, and a territorial and industrial vision of development would be used to facilitate the global integration of markets and centres of population in order to stem the spread of poverty in major cities.
(b) Based on the findings of these studies, analyse the range of feasible, necessary, and advisable interconnections, determining the entry dates and the investments required.
(c) Make audits of each country's reserves, establishing the foreseeable supply-and-demand balances and estimating the reserves each country needs to discover, in order to evaluate the cost/benefits and balances among them and the supply security, vis-à-vis the advantages of integration.
(d) Outline and move ahead with agreements on financing mechanisms, price policies, and trust fund management, in order to ensure upstream and downstream investments. State-owned corporations can contribute to this objective by using oil revenues rationally.
(e) Establish administrative mechanisms and the responsibilities of the future regional supranational regulating agency or equivalent body.
(f) Analyse methodologies for rate-setting and rules for the open access, supply security, competition, and protection of investments of users, in order to establish in the mid-term the initial drafts of the common regulatory frameworks to be studied in-depth and negotiated by the different countries and actors in the system.

246. 'Energy clusters'. Unlike trade in primary and secondary forms of energy – a typical commodities trade –, whose prices have followed a downward trend of long standing, trade in energy services and in the capital goods required for the industry enjoy larger profit margins. These are high value added goods and services.

247. Therein lies the importance of devising strategies for energy-based participation in the world economy that go beyond taking advantage of primary and secondary energy trade opportunities to assume an energy cluster approach.

248. No systematic information is available today in the Andean countries that breaks down energy cluster activities sufficiently and at the same time makes their interrelationship possible. It was for that reason that the First Meeting of the Council of Andean Community Ministers of Energy, Electricity, Hydrocarbons, and Mines, held in Quito in January 2004, gave priority to this area of work and agreed that UNCTAD would provide technical assistance for its development.

249. Renewable energy sources and their tie-in with the Environmental theme and with the PIDS. The First Meeting of the Council of Andean Community Ministers of Energy, Electricity, Hydrocarbons, and Mines underscored the importance of linking up renewable energy sources with the implementation of the Andean Community's PIDS.

250. The launching of studies was proposed to give special priority to the use of renewable energy sources in anti-poverty programmes and to foster access to basic services and their intensive use for meeting energy requirements in border, isolated, and rural areas and, in general, of the population lacking energy sources.

251. The First Meeting of energy and environment experts on the topic of renewable energy sources, held in Lima in May 2004, for its part, identified the following criteria for deepening the analysis of renewable energy sources in the Subregion:

(a) The Subregion's renewable energy potential can play a key role in the world energy system by guaranteeing sustainable development and its ability to create new forms of cooperation among developing countries and between these and developed countries within the context of international environmental conservation commitments.
(b) New strategies and policies must be put into play that will allow for rational use of endogenous energy sources and enable new and renewable sources to contribute to the security of the energy supply, while considering the particular needs of the individual Member Countries.
(c) Renewable energy sources constitute an asset for negotiation and their development can open up new opportunities for investment in local and regional development.
(d) Despite the advances made in electricity coverage in the Andean Subregion, nearly 22 million people continue to live in isolated communities without electrical services. Renewable energy sources can help enormously to provide those communities with sustainable electric power and other forms of energy.
(e) Inasmuch as access to energy sources helps improve the living conditions of people in the Subregion, it is essential to link up this theme with the formulation and implementation of the PIDS/Decision 553, in keeping with the United Nations' Millennium Development goals.
(f) It is important to evaluate the role renewable energy sources can play in the provision of energy and the productive development of the integration hubs in which the Andean Community is involved within the framework of the SARII.
(g) The Andean Community should play an active role within the Johannesburg Renewable Energy Coalition.

The meeting concluded by identifying the need to lay the groundwork for a future Andean Renewable Energy Strategy to be considered at the next meeting of the Council of Andean Ministers of Energy, Electricity, Hydrocarbons, and Mines.

§6. Integration and Border Development

252. From the beginning of the Andean Subregion constitution in 1969, the land frontiers have been a relevant issue for the community and especially for the Member Countries.

It was always thought that the functionality of the public institutions located at the main border crossings had to be adapted to create the favourable conditions that would allow for the unobstructed movement of people, goods, cargo, and passenger vehicles in international traffic to the interior of the subregional territory.[21]

253. With this criterion, there was an opinion within the Cartagena Agreement that Member Countries would develop joint actions to achieve a better utilization of the physical space, strengthen infrastructure and the necessary services for the advancement of the economic process of integration in the subregion.

254. This objective would be carried out mainly in the energy fields, transportation, and communications, and it would include the necessary measures to facilitate border traffic among Member Countries. This argument was maintained throughout the years, for the objective was still the equal. The reasoning establishes a fundamental coherence between the progressive structuring and functioning of the subregional market and the border institutional adjustment according to the demands of free bidirectional circulation of connected services, mainly land transport.

I. Borders

255. The zones of border constitute for the Andean Community the geographic areas, natural and privileged of joint of the economies and societies of the four Member Countries. They are, also, the point of contact of the national road networks through which important part of the commercial and tourist interchange is made.

256. Considering this, the Andean countries adopted, by means of Decision 459, the Communitarian Policy for Integration and the Border Development, as an essential component of the fortification and consolidation of the process of subregional and regional integration. The main target of this policy is to elevate the quality of life of the populations and the development of its institutions, within the border territorial scopes between the countries of the CAN.

257. Group of High-Level. In order to guarantee the instrumentation of the Communitarian Policy, the work group of High-Level for Integration and Border Development was created, integrated by the competent national authorities in this matter, with the order to propose the programmes and plans of action. The coordination of this group is in charge of the Outer Cabinet of Relations, whereas the technical secretariat exerts the General Secretariat of the CAN. By recommendation of this Work group, the Andean Council of Ministers of Outer Relations confirmed Decisions 501 and 502, referred to the BIZ and the Binational Centers of Attention in Border (BCAB), respectively.

258. The BIZ and the BCAB. The BIZ, settles down with the purpose of generating optimal conditions for integration, and the sustainable border development between the Member Countries of the CAN. Their objectives are to contribute to diversify, to fortify, and to stabilize economic, social, cultural, institutional, and political bonds between the Andean countries; to favour the local authorities, harnessing its productive, commercial, and cultural capacities; to contribute to deepen the national processes of economic and administrative decentralization, among others.

The Binational Border Assistance Centers (CEBAF) must objectively implant a system that is efficient and integrated of management and control of the bidirectional

---

21. *See* Andean Community website: www.comunidadandina.org, Infrastructure and borders.

traffics that are canalized by the border passages – to avoid the duplicity of proceedings; to carry out in the CEBAF the registry of the information on the flow of people, luggage, merchandise, and vehicles, among others. Members of the CAN by means of specific agreements could be established by the countries, in agreement with the characteristics and peculiarities of their respective passages of border.

II. Intracommunity Migrations

259. The Andean countries have decided to add efforts to obtain that their inhabitants can circulate freely in the subregion, or when they do it for reasons of tourism, of work or aims that imply change of habitual residence.

260. Temporal migration or of short duration. The Outer Cabinet of Relations in the past years sent a series of communitarian Decisions that they look for to guarantee the free circulation of people in the territories of the Member Countries. In June 2001, it was approved of Decision 503 that it recognizes national documents of identification as only a requirement, so that the resident nationals and foreigners in the Member Countries can travel in the subregion as tourists. In September 2006, the Andean Card of Migration was approved by means of Resolution 527 of the General Secretariat of the CAN (TAM) as uniform document of migratory and statistical control of obligatory use, for the entry and exit of people of the territory of the Member Countries.

261. Permanent migration or long play. In June 2003, by means of Decision 545, the Andean Instrument of Labour Migration that contemplates to norms for the progressive and gradual circulation and permanence of Andean nationals in the Subregion was adopted, with labour aims under dependency relation, in conditions of equality of treatment and opportunities. This norm is still not regulated.

262. In May 2004, it was established by means of Decision 583, the Andean Instrument of Social Security that looks for to guarantee the suitable social protection of the labour migrants and its beneficiaries so that, as a result of the migration, they do not see decreased social rights. This same date settled down, by means of Decision 584 the Andean Instrument of Security and Health in the work. This Decision 583 is not regulated; however, 584 is.

263. Also, by means of Decisions 399, 439, 510 and other tie ins, the countries of the CAN guarantee the circulation of employees of the lending companies, as well as the crew of the lending companies of the transport service.

III. Extracommunity Migrations

264. The communitarian action in the matter of migrations towards third countries is centred, mainly, in offering to the Maxima protection and attendance to the migrants in the territories of third countries. The efforts of the countries to improve the identification of their nationals are important and to contribute to the subject of the border security, perfecting their administrative systems corresponding to the public registries and of identification of people.

265. A significant step in that sense occurred when Decisions 504 that creates the Andean Passport and 525 that establishes the 'technical Characteristics specific minims of nomenclature and security of the Andean Passport' incorporating the recommendations of the Civil Aviation International Organization (CAIO) were adopted.

266. The CFP orchestrated by the Andean Council of Outer Ministers of Relations anticipates the adoption of joint positions in the specialized international forums. A departure point is the document of work advanced in previous years by the SGCAN on the Guidelines of the CFP of Migrations of the Andean Community.

267. In 2003, it approved, by means of Decision 548, Mechanism Andean of Cooperation in the matter of Attendance and Protection Consular in Subjects Migratory, which establishes that all national of Member Country of Andean Community, which is in the territory of a third State, in which its country of origin does not have Diplomatic or Consular Representation, will be able to take refuge in the protection of the diplomatic or consular authorities of any other Member Country. The total implementation of this instrument is still pending to complete itself.

268. In negotiations CAN-EU, one looks for to register the migratory subject in the political pillar in the Agreement of Association. In the Agreement of Political Dialogue and Cooperation of 2003, the 'illegal migration' is mentioned solely. The Andean proposal talks about the importance of the migration for the development of the States Part in the Agreement of Association, to the promotion and protection of the human rights – independently of its migratory quality the elimination of the discrimination, xenophobia and exclusion, social integration and cultural, the facilities of the shipment of remittances, the combat to deal with its people, and among other subjects, the combat to the illicit traffic of migrants. The migratory subject will be due, consequently, to deal with integral and comprehensive way.

During the fourth Andean migrations forum developed in Bogota on 9 and 10 May, discussions were initiated regarding the project of 'Andean Migratory Regulation', which will try to consolidate, in a single communitarian norm, the rights of circulation and residence of Andean citizens on the communitarian space. Equally, this project tries to create conditions for the construction of a South American space with equal migratory norms, which will be integrated advances in the same direction as other multinational instances, especially UNASUR and the European Union.

§7. Socio-Labour Matters

269. This key subject area is being developed within the framework of the PIDS Project 'Andean Subregional Employment Promotion Program' – Decision 601.

270. Although employment generation depends basically on economic growth and the technological characteristics of the production sectors responsible for that growth, it is possible to design policy instruments that will improve the relationship between labour supply and demand, promote specific production activities that have a greater capacity to create jobs than others, identify job and income generating possibilities to be found in resolving Community problems and needs, and raise the productivity and income-generating levels of small-scale production activities, etc. An exchange of successful experiences with these and other initiatives could make a considerable contribution to the store of instruments and policy measures available to formulate national employment promotion policies.

271. Furthermore, the gradual formulation of an Andean subregional framework of employment promotion policies could be highly useful as a common reference point for formulating and building up national employment promotion policies in a context of growing economic interdependence brought on by the advance of Andean integration.

272. Collect, evaluate, and systematically organize the experiences of the Member Countries in this area and establish a Community framework to boost the formulation of employment promotion policies, with special emphasis on the informal urban sector and the promotion of micro-, small-, and medium-size enterprises (SMEs).

273. The following lines of work have been developed in the area of employment:

(1) Orchestrate an exchange among Andean countries of successful experiences with national employment promotion policies and programmes, including national systems of cooperatives.
(2) Step up Andean mutual technical cooperation among the subregion's Labour Ministries.
(3) Within the framework of the Andean Regional Employment Conferences initiative, foster a subregional debate on the coordination of economic and social policies in order to support the formulation of employment policies conceived as State policies.
(4) Promote tripartite social dialogue within the context of the Simón Rodríguez Convention, in order to produce consensual initiatives for increasing employment sources that offer decent jobs.
(5) Further increased intersector and inter-Ministry coordination within the subregion for strengthening the role of Labour Ministries as the guiding bodies for national employment policies.
(6) Ensure the active participation of the Advisory Council of Labour Ministers and of the Andean Labour and Business Advisory Councils in the formulation of a future decision on Andean employment promotion.
(7) Foster the involvement of the labour and business sectors in the design, execution, and evaluation of national policies to reactivate production and promote employment.

§8. Democracy and Human Rights

I. Democracy

274. The Andean Community Member Countries have demonstrated their democratic vocation ever since the founding of the integration process in 1969, as can be seen in its supreme law, the Cartagena Agreement, which is grounded in 'the principles of equality, justice, peace, solidarity, and democracy'.

275. These democratic convictions have been reaffirmed over the years in a variety of pronouncements, such as the Andean countries' contribution to the overthrow of the Somoza dictatorship in Nicaragua and their rejection of the attempt by Colonel Natush Bush to overthrow the Bolivian Government.

276. A further expression of that vocation were the efforts of Colombia, Peru, and Venezuela to secure peace and democracy in Central America through the CONTADORA and Support Groups backed by the Andean Group, which later gave way to the creation of the Political Consultation and Coordination Mechanism, initially known as the Group of Eight and, as of its enlargement, as the Group of Río.

277. In 1980, when the rule of law had been re-established in all of the Andean countries, the Andean Presidents, in Riobamba, Ecuador, signed the Code of Conduct establishing the democratic nature of the Subregion's political systems, together with the Member Countries' commitment to respect human, political, economic, and social rights as their basic norm of national behaviour.

278. Among the more recent events, attention should be drawn to the Declaration of the Andean Council of Presidents on Democracy and Integration, signed in Bogotá on 7 August 1998, during Andrés Pastrana's Presidential inauguration.

279. That Declaration reiterates CAN's commitment to democracy by establishing that 'the Andean Community is a community of democratic nations' and 'that among its main objectives are the development and consolidation of democracy and the rule of law, as well as respect for human rights and basic freedoms'(Declaration of the Andean Council of Presidents on Democracy and Integration (Bogotá, Colombia, 1998)).

280. The promotion and defence of democracy is a key issue on the Andean Community's Foreign Policy Agenda. In effect, the exercise of democracy resting on the participation of the citizens and social justice is among the major principles of Decision 458, whereby the Andean Council of Foreign Ministers approved the 'Common Foreign Policy Guidelines', and its main objectives include the development and consolidation of democracy and the rule of law, as well as the promotion of, and respect for, human rights and basic freedoms.

281. Along this same line, an area of CFP action in the political terrain is the affirmation of democracy as a requirement for consolidation of the subregion's integration process and for helping to strengthen democracy and human rights through the Andean Community's international dialogue and cooperation activities.

282. The Andean Council of Foreign Ministers, at the request of the Andean Presidents, drew up a draft Additional Protocol to the Cartagena Agreement, the 'Andean Community Commitment to Democracy.' Four of the Member Countries signed this document in Oporto, Portugal, on 17 October 1998 and the last one signed it at the Twelfth Meeting of the Andean Council of Presidents on 9 and 10 June 2000.

283. The Protocol stipulates that 'the full effectiveness of the democratic institutions and the rule of law' are an essential precondition for political cooperation and integration and indicates the procedures to be followed in the event that the democratic order is disrupted in any of the Member Countries.

284. Those measures range from the suspension of the country's participation in any of the bodies of the Andean Integration System and its 'ineligibility to accede to the facilities or loans of the Andean financial institutions', to the 'suspension of rights deriving from the Cartagena Agreement and the coordination of external measures in other spheres'(Additional Protocol to the Cartagena Agreement, the 'Andean Community Commitment to Democracy').

285. Drawing their inspiration from this Protocol and from the Southern Common Market's 1998 Protocol of Usuaia, the Presidents of the Andean Community and the MERCOSUR countries approved, on 1 September 2000 in the city of Brasilia, the so-called democratic clause in paragraph 23 of the Communiqué, which states that 'Maintenance of the rule of law and full respect for the democratic system in each of the twelve countries of the region constitute an objective and a shared commitment, which as of today is a prerequisite for participation in future South American meetings.'(Statement of Brasilia Meeting of Presidents of South America, Brasilia, 1 September 2000). The Presidents went on to add that 'Respecting the existing regional mechanisms, they agreed, in that connection, to hold political consultations if a disruption of the democratic order in South America is threatened.'

286. This 'South American democratic clause' is a key element for the integration of this community of democratic nations in South America and commits them to the exercise of democracy and the rule of law in the region.

287. At their March 2001 meeting in Lima, the Andean Community Foreign Ministers reiterated their countries' strong democratic vocation and agreed upon the need to further strengthen the institutions and to promote respect for human rights.

288. After underscoring the importance of the application of the 'Andean Community Commitment to Democracy', the Foreign Ministers reiterated their support for Peru's initiative to adopt an 'Inter-American Democratic Charter'. This was accomplished on 11 September 2001, during the Special General Assembly of the Organization of American States, in Lima.

289. Furthermore, our leaders, at the Thirteenth Andean Council of Presidents, held in Valencia, Venezuela on 23 and 24 June 2001, reiterated their firm intent to continue strengthening democratic rule in the Andean countries. They agreed that the democratic governance of their respective countries is an absolute priority and, accordingly, reiterated their commitment to resolve, by constitutional means, any temporary difficulty that could arise in the Andean region.

290. The Heads of State, moreover, in the Machu Picchu Declaration on Democracy, the Rights of Indigenous Peoples and the War against Poverty, signed on 29 July 2001, on the occasion of Alejandro Toledo's Presidential inauguration in Peru, expressed their firm conviction that democracy, development, and respect for human rights and basic freedoms are interdependent and mutually strengthening. In this connection, they reiterated their intention to reinforce democracy as a system of government and as an irreplaceable element of our political identity, to promote democratic values as a way of life and to defend democratic institutions and the rule of law in Latin America and the Caribbean. They further reaffirmed that the effective exercise of democracy requires the strengthening of its participatory nature.

II. Human Rights

291. As pointed out above, an immediate precedent to be considered is the Riobamba Code of Conduct, signed on 11 September 1980 by the Presidents of

Colombia, Ecuador, Venezuela, and the Personal Representative of the President of Peru.

292. In that document, the Andean countries reaffirmed that respect for human, political, economic, and social rights is a fundamental domestic rule of conduct of the Andean States and that its defence is an international obligation, to which the Status are bound, and that, as a result, joint action taken to protect those rights does not violate the principle of non-intervention.

293. It should be recalled that the Andean countries have been promoters and signers of most of the international instruments for the protection and promotion of human rights, within both the United Nations and the Organization of American States, and this has become an important basis for the designing of a Community policy on the subject.

294. Among the notable instruments in which the Andean countries have played a significant role is the 1993 Vienna Declaration and Plan of Action. Its key principles include the responsibility of the international community for promoting and defending human rights, the holistic conception of those rights, and the connection between democracy, human rights, and development.

295. The Andean Presidents have followed this course of international pronouncements at their consecutive annual meetings of the Andean Council of Presidents. At the Thirteenth Andean Council of Presidents in Valencia, Venezuela, on 23 and 24 June 2001, our leaders announced their decision to approve an Andean Human Rights Charter to ensure the effective exercise of human rights, reinforce democratic governance and the rule of law, and firmly establish a culture of peace in the Andean nations.

296. They, accordingly, instructed the Andean Council of Foreign Ministers to draw up this Charter, which was to contain the principles and main lines of a Community policy on the subject and a cooperation programme to expedite specific actions aimed at ensuring the observance of, and respect for, those rights in the Andean region, within the framework of the 1980 American Human Rights Convention and the Riobamba Code of Conduct.

297. The intention was for this Andean Charter to, among other things, strengthen the rule of law and improve the administration of justice; promote a culture of peace through dialogue, tolerance, and concerted decisions, as social consensus-building instruments; reinforce the right to development; and build up institutions for the defence and promotion of human rights in the Member Countries, particularly the Offices of the Ombudsmen.

298. In the cited Machu Picchu Declaration on Democracy, the Rights of Indigenous Peoples and the War against Poverty, signed on July 2001, for its part, the Presidents renewed their governments' commitment to the exercise of, and respect for, human rights.

299. They also reiterated their will to strengthen the Inter-American Human Rights System, including the possibility of the progressively permanent operation of the Inter-American Court of Human Rights and the Inter-American Human Rights Commission, and to foster the universality of the Inter-American system for the protection of human rights.

300. It is important to draw attention to the Presidents' support for all efforts to promote and protect the fundamental rights and freedoms of the indigenous peoples, among them: the right to their own spiritual, cultural, and linguistic identity and traditions; their social, political, cultural, and economic rights; their right, as peoples, not to be divested of their historical, cultural heritage; their right to their systems and knowledge of traditional medicine and to its practice, including the right to protection of their ritual sites and sacred places; their right to an education that respects their differences; and the right to be elected to and to hold public office.

301. The Heads of State also expressed their intention to safeguard these rights within the public order and in compliance with existing constitutional and legal provisions, among other significant agreements.

302. It is important to emphasize here that the Andean Council of Foreign Ministers, at its Twelfth Regular Meeting, held on 7 May 2004 in Guayaquil, Ecuador, adopted Decision 586 'Working Program for the Dissemination and Execution of the Andean Charter for the Promotion and Protection of Human Rights' that establishes specific goals for the Promotion of the Andean Charter; for its national and international implementation; for its follow-up; and for its projection in the medium and short terms. In addition, it contains a general timetable and indicates ways to seek the financing needed for the program's implementation.

303. As a result of that Programme, the Andean Charter is available in Quechua and Shuar, prepared by the Ministry of Foreign Affairs of Ecuador, and in Spanish, from the Andean Labour Advisory Council.

Chapter 4. CAN Challenges

304. Taking the Guidance Principles and the Andean Strategic Agenda approved on 5 February 2010 as a reference, the Declaration made by the VII Andean Social Development Ministers Council (CADS) that took place in Lima, Peru on 6 July 2011, in which eleven Andean Social Development Objectives and their corresponding goals to be reached by 2019, as well as the Andean Economical and Social Cohesion Strategies were established, twelve priority points that make up the challenges that the Member Countries have decided to face together can be defined and will be expanded upon next.

§1. Citizen Participation

305. In different norms and actions by the Andean Community, the importance of citizen participation is acknowledged and the encouragement and strengthening of working and collaboration relationships between civil society organizations of the Member Countries through the development of joint projects is contemplated; as well as the gradual development of an organized citizen participation practice in decision-making process about integration, within the framework of the SAI. One of the governing principles stated in the Andean Strategic Agenda is, precisely, 'to promote the citizen participation in the integration process'(Andean Strategic Agenda, Lima, Peru, 2010).

The organized citizen participation in the Andean integration process is carried out through the Advisory Council, which is entitled to present their points of view to the organs of the SAI and is actively engaged, with right to speak, at meetings related to the subregional integration process.

306. Experiences such as the action with the SOCICAN,[22] the work done by subregional networks, the participation of Native People in the Andean Integration System, and the work done by the African-descendant people show progress in this field, and yet there is still much to be done. Within this context, the strategic actions to be taken by the CAN in this field follow three main lines:

22. That promotes mechanisms and interaction spaces between different groups and organizations from civil society around the topics of environment, human rights, peace culture, and territorial development, as well as communication for development, amongst other subjects.

- to strengthen the participation of civil society organizations (schools, universities, research institutions, etc.) in the SAI and in the communal actions of the Andean Community institutionalizing its representative participation within it;
- to consolidate and evaluate the undergoing projects to incorporate new civil society participation practices and projects; and
- to institutionalize the periodical high-level dialogue between the SAI bodies and institutions.

It should be stated that in the Declaration made by the VII Andean Social Development Ministers Council that took place on 6 July 2011, reducing the social inequities that affect the indigenous and African-descended people through the encouragement of their participation was established as a CAN objective.

With respect of the indigenous peoples, the creation of the Advisory Council of Indigenous Peoples of the Andean Community (CCPICAN) (Decision 674), in 2007, marked the beginning of a series of actions aimed at promoting the active participation of indigenous peoples in matters related to subregional integration in their economic, social, cultural, and political fields. Thus, after an initial period of organization that included the election of Representatives from Indigenous Organizations, it is passed to the development and adoption, within the framework of national workshops, of the Strategic Plan of CCPICAN containing topics articulators, which will strengthen its permanent action, which include:

- Indigenous Peoples;
- Climate change;
- Land and territory (Rights of peoples, nationalities, and mother earth);
- Management and organizational impact;
- Political participation (Participation and influence in regional and national public policy);
- Right to consultation and prior consent;
- Economic policies, integration, and 'Good Life';
- The criminalization of indigenous social conflicts and persecution;

Participation of indigenous women (Rights and Promotion of women and indigenous family).Among the activities that are being implemented are the following:

- Promotion of Andean rights on the basis of the Andean Charter for the Promotion and Protection of Human Rights;
- Construction of the 'Andean Indigenous Peoples Program';
- Creation of the 'Andean Committee of Government Authorities on the Rights of Indigenous Peoples';
- Consolidation of the Andean Association of Indigenous Peoples and Intercultural Communities;
- Development of proposals on issues of common interest;
- Promotion CCPICAN positioning in different spaces;
- Development of Indigenous Peoples Directory.

As for people of African descendant by Decision 758 in 2011, the Bureau of African Descendants of the Andean Community was created to promote the active participation of their representative organizations in matters related to subregional integration. It consists of two representatives of African descendant of each Member Country of the Andean Community, a delegate of government and a delegate of the Ombudsman of each of the Andean countries.

Amongst its functions are those of issue opinions to the competent organs of the Andean Community on issues related to people of African descendant; promote respect and guarantee their rights; maintain working relationships with organizations and agencies of the Andean Integration System (SAI) to develop the Afro agenda in Andean region and promote joint actions for comprehensive integration and the well-being of the Andean Community; among others.

Ongoing activities are:

- The completion of the process of accreditation of representatives of the Member Countries of the Andean Community.
- Conducting the first meeting of the Bureau of African Descendants Participation, CAN.
- Coordination and approval of the Andean Program for Afro-descendant Participation in the Andean Integration.
- Performing consulting ethno education in the framework of Andean integration.
- Socialization of communication products: (a) the Andean legislation on the protection of the rights of African descendant; (b) publication of the Andean ranges of African descendant rule participation in Andean integration; (c) Priorities Sheet for Andean peoples of African descent.
- Elaboration of the Directory of national organizations and civil society organizations working in the development and protection of the rights of Afro-descendants in the countries of the Andean Community.

The goals set on this regard, and whose progressive fulfilment is foreseen until the year 2019, are: to improve by 50% the access to basic services (water, sanitation, electricity) of the indigenous and African-descendant people; as well as accomplishing that 100% of the indigenous and African-descendant population has an identification document.

§2. Common Foreign Policy

One of the Andean integration objectives acknowledged by the Cartagena Agreement is to facilitate the participation of the Member Countries in the regional integration process and to tend to diminish the external vulnerability and to improve the position of the countries in the international economic context.

To this regard, the Andean Community has expanded and diversified its international relationships, placing special emphasis in intensifying the relationships with Latin America and the Caribbean in political and economical dimensions, favouring the strengthening of the political dialogue and the cooperation with other countries and institutions in accordance to the CFP Lineaments stated in Decision 458.

The CAN has, amongst its main objectives, to strengthen the CFP through the Andean participation in regional integration initiatives and models, the convergence with current integration processes, the consolidation of relationships with Latin American countries, the broadening of extra-regional relationships with Europe, Asia-Pacific, the US, Mexico, Panama, and the political dialogue and cooperation with China, Russia, and India.

To that effect, the CFP actions identified in Decision 458 are the following: Political Area, Economic Area, and Socio-Cultural Area.

Political Area: Execution of actions directed to consolidate regional unity; the improvement of extra-regional relationships, the affirmation, consolidation and strengthening of democracy, and respect of human rights; the strengthening of multilateralism as a means to promote dialogue, consensus and international cooperation, the assurance of the strict adherence to international law, and the neutralization of unilateral and extraterritorial actions.

Also, the promotion of a culture of peace and of peaceful controversy resolution and the promotion of trust, the limitation of armaments and the development of new regional concepts of democratic security.

This area also contemplates the boost of Sustainable Development Policies, especially in the area of environmental preservation and biodiversity defence; the undergoing of joint actions against the worldwide drug problem, as well as the adoption of mechanism for cooperation and social control aimed at the fighting and eradication of corruption, terrorism, and the illicit arms trade.

307. Economic Area: Execution of actions directed to the articulation and convergence of the existing integration models in the region, with the objective of the formation of a common Latin American market; the promotion of free trade; the preservation and the development of preferential access mechanisms established in favour of Andean Community countries; the strengthening of international cooperation; the promotion of commerce and investments.

Also, the promotion of commerce of goods and services is desired; the execution of effective foreign investment policies; the continuation of a joint stand on intellectual property; the establishment of a long-term community agricultural policy, and, in regards to international financing, the strengthening of stability, the increase of financial flows, and the reduction of the vulnerability of the region's economies to external unbalances.

This area also takes into account the development of energy resources and the promotion, strengthening, and diversification of transport services to empower the relationships with the other subregional and regional models, as well as the economic ties in the international setting of the Andean countries.

308. Socio-cultural area: Execution of actions directed at strengthening, promoting, and consolidating the Latin American identity, as well as the rights of the indigenous populations; the preservation, prevention, and fight against international contraband consisting of artefacts and goods belonging to the historical, cultural, and archaeological patrimony of Andean countries, and the diffusion of the Andean cultural patrimony.

309. Also, on the Andean Strategic Agenda, the following are stated as CAN challenges in regards to Foreign Relationships:

- To promote the permanent and proactive participation in the initiatives, spaces, and models of regional integration (on a South American, UNASUR and Latin American level), the Community of Latin American and Caribbean States (CELAC).
- To converge with MERCOSUR activities to coordinate and strengthen the Latin American integration through the establishment of a Joint CAN-MERCOSUR Commission.
- To deepen the relationships with Chile and other associated members to the Andean Community.
- To consolidate the relationships with Mexico and Panama.
- To establish a permanent dialogue with the Central American Integration System (SICA and SIECA).
- To implement the mechanisms for political dialogue and cooperation with China, Russia, and India.
- To deepen the political dialogue and cooperation with the European Union.
- To promote the dialogue and cooperation with the US.
- To insert the Andean Community in the Asia-Pacific region.
- To regulate the Andean Cooperation Mechanism regarding Consular Assistance and Protection and Migratory Matters (Decision 548).

§3. Economical and Commercial Integration

310. The CAN, for purposes of promoting its balanced and harmonic development, will facilitate commerce, encourage production, and promote the exports and consumption on a regional scale.

311. To this end, SME-related programmes are developed, increasing the support to small- and micro-sized enterprises on an Andean-level, implementing tools for their strengthening, contacting, and productive complementation; as well as commerce and goods production; commercial origin and defence; customs, quality and sanitation, macroeconomics and tariff policies, intellectual property and services; competition and customers.

312. Likewise, support is meant to be provided for public policies regarding science, technology, and innovation through specific actions oriented to strengthen competitiveness and complementarities in the subregion.

313. The communal management also seeks to deepen the commercial integration, consolidating and perfecting the existing Andean free trade zone, aiming to facilitate the free circulation of goods and to increase the commercial productivity and capacity of the Member Countries, keeping updated the List of Goods Manufactured (NBNP), and establishing the reference prices of the products that make up the Andean Band System Price. It further highlights the actions of implementation and commissioning of the computer System of ARIAN, as well as technical assistance to Member Countries in their trade information systems.

314. There are four large areas to be developed on this subject.

I. Production, Commerce, and Sustainable Consumption

315. The actions to be developed in this category seek to strengthen Andean commerce according to what is established in the Cartagena Accord.

316. Within this framework, initiatives that favour small producers will be fomented, promoting fair and supportive commerce amongst other ways of promoting economic and social inclusion, as well as the social, environmental, and technological responsibility of economic ventures.

317. Also, with respect for the national regulatory framework of each Member Country, bio-commerce will be promoted under criteria of environmental, social, and economical sustainability and the sustainable consumption of products derived from productive processes generated with economical, social, and environmental profitability.

II. Promotion of Production

318. In this context, the creation and support of operations of regional and Andean-level companies will be promoted, oriented to the production of goods and services, of both the Andean market and other countries.

319. To that effect, tools that contribute to the creation and strengthening of Andean SMEs, their productive networking and complementation, and their participation in the Andean market will be designed and implemented.

320. *324*. Also, the operation of a Regional Network of Science and Technology will be promoted, as well as the complementation of productive chains, especially in the agricultural sector and the identification of a selection of Andean products, which empower its offering capacity in the markets.

III. Economic Complementation

321. Amongst the main actions to be performed is the promoting of economic association and complementation with inclusive participation of all the involved sectors, evaluating the Andean common regulations in matters of investment protection and promotion, as well as the potential for establishing an Andean regulation for the public purchasing of goods.

322. Parallel to this, it is expected to strengthen the Andean System for Agricultural Sanitation; the Andean Quality System – evaluating the establishment of the Andean System of Food Safety; the Macroeconomical Convergence Programmes; and the continuation of exchange of information and studies of the Andean agenda, aimed at preventing and facing the international economic crisis.

IV. Commercial Integration

323. In this aspect, the current actions to achieve the consolidation of the free circulation of goods, services, and people, considering the national regulations of each

Member Country, and the projects related to an Andean Community Tariff Policy, will be continued.

324. Also, an Andean strategy to identify markets, facilitate commerce, encourage production, and promote exports and regional-scale usage will be developed and the development of an Andean regulation, which promotes commerce, will be continued.

§4. Physical Integration and Border Development

In December 2009, the Andean Community Committee adopted Decisions 724 and 725, which centre on the operation and commercialization of the OSR of the Andean countries on position 67° West, having signed a contract for the commercial usage of the Andean satellite position, directing the actions towards the development of the mechanisms for the administration of it to the effect of reactivating the satellite position and maintaining the OSR operational.

Also listed on the agenda is the promotion of integration of the telecommunication sector, such as roaming services in border regions; the convergence of networks and telecommunications services, the telecommunication networks for the prevention, attention, and mitigation of natural disasters; the development of broadband and the sharing of data of stolen mobile devices in the subregion.

In regards to transportation, it is currently considered a priority action to define the treatment that will be given to Decision 399 regarding Highway Merchandise Transportation.

Other relevant action is the diffusion of Decision 619, 'Regulations for the Harmonization of Rights and Obligations of User, Transporters and Operators of the Air Transportation Services in the Andean Community', which is of high impact for the citizens of Member Countries.

In regards to physical infrastructure, the necessary actions to review Decision 271 'Andean Highway System' will be undertaken, aiming at its updating and the consolidation of the Andean Highway System. Also, the development and modernization of transportation activities (on highways, airways, waterways, railways, and multimode), electrical and telecommunications interconnection of the Member Countries; the development of the Andean integration and physical (ports, airports, and river transport) interconnection system and the promotion of ease of access to ports are listed as challenges.

In the case of border development, the actions are mainly directed at supporting the development of binational border projects prioritized by the Member Countries. For this, the cooperation of the European Union, the Spanish Agency for International Cooperation (AECID), and the Inter-American Development Bank (BID) is available.

Likewise, it was planned to support the construction of CEBAF. Member Countries, in pairs of countries, are making progress in the establishment of the CEBAF. In that sense:

– Between Bolivia and Peru, a temporary CEBAF of Desaguadero and the feasibility study and final design of the final CEBAF at that border crossing will soon begin.

- Colombia and Ecuador have identified technical needs and investments necessary to enable the operation of CEBAF juxtaposed in the vicinity of the bridge of Rumichaca, on the basis of existing CEBAF Ipiales (Colombia) and Tulcán (Ecuador).
- Ecuador and Peru are working together to define the place where the CEBAF of Huaquillas -Aguas Verdes will be established. The studies are funded by the European Union. It also has been a progress in the approval of customs and immigration procedures and harmonization of hours of operation.
- Between Colombia and Venezuela, technical meetings have been held in order to establish the CEBAF Paraguachón in La Guajira sector. Likewise, the implementation of integrated border control is planned to promote the development of BIZ and to start the procedures meant to increase the financing resources to deepen the integration on the borders of the Andean countries, amongst others, through the strengthening of the Bank for Integration and Border Development Projects (BPIF).

325. Some other challenges in this area include: to establish a permanent financial mechanism, which allows the execution of binational projects of border development; to encourage the creation of Andean multinational enterprises in the BIZ, in the production of goods, offering of services and the promotion of investments, and in its complementation, specially at a sector level; and in promoting public and public-private actions destined to reduce economic inequality and asymmetry in border zones.

326. In the Declaration made by the VII Andean Social Development Ministers Council that took place in Lima, Peru, on 6 July 2011, it was established as a CAN objective to promote social development in depressed areas, particularly in mainly rural and border areas, to the effect of accomplishing the following goals by 2019: to reduce economic poverty and extreme poverty rate by 40% in the rural area; and to improve the access to basic services (water, sanitation, electricity) of border populations by 50%.

§5. Social Development

327. In the Quirama Presidential Summit, XIVth Meeting of the Andean Presidential Council, which took place in the year 2003, it was agreed:

> to grant maximum priority to the design, coordination and convergence of social policies that lead to the development of specific and articulated social cohesion and fight against poverty and exclusion strategies that contribute to the consolidation of democracy and the strengthening of governability in the Andean Community, as well as the generation of broader spaces for the participation of social actors and organizations.[23]

23. XIV Meeting of the Andean Presidential Council, which took place in Quirama, Colombia, in June 2003.

It was also established to prioritize the approval of the PIDS as a complement to the national development plans.

328. In this context, the CAN initiated an ambitious Andean Social Agenda that initially encompasses the following thematic axis: (a) Social dimension of the integration process; (b) Community action to contribute to improve the quality of life of the Andean inhabitants; (c) Citizen participation in the integration process.

329. In the year 2004, the PIDS – Decision 601 – was adopted, which constitutes the largest-scale proposal within the second axis of the aforementioned Andean Social Agenda. The PIDS, taken as a community social strategy, has the purpose of channelling actions of subregional reach (activities, projects, and programmes), which enriches and complements the national policies to overcome poverty and social inequity.[24]

330. The Andean Council of Social Development Ministers, National PIDs Committee, Andean Network of NGOs, and academic entities are in charge of the execution of the PIDS.

331. From that date on, the design and implementation of a set of social-labour, poverty, exclusion, inequality and asymmetry overcoming projects, food safety, health, education and culture, environment, rural and border development, amongst others. To this end, subregional programmes aimed at social development are being executed with the objective of strengthening the national efforts aimed at the completion of these goals.

332. Therefore, in regards to *overcoming poverty and inequality*, in the Declaration made by the VII Andean Social Development Ministers Council that took place in Lima, Peru, on 6 July 2011, it was established as a goal for the CAN, the eradication and reduction of economic and social inequalities. To this end, as goals to be accomplished progressively until the year 2019, are listed: to reduce, by one-third, the monetary extreme poverty; by at least 40% the total monetary poverty; by at least 10% the Gini coefficient of per capita household income;[25] and, by half, the occurrence of monetary poverty in indigenous and African-descendant people.

Respect rural development. The Agriculture Ministers of the Member Countries of the Andean Community adopted in June 2013 Guidelines and Strategic Objectives for Rural Territorial Development of the Andean Community, which will guide the joint work at the subregional level in this area. An Andean Rural Territorial Development Committee was set up for the formulation, fundraising, and monitoring of a Subregional Integrated Program for Rural Territorial Development. They also recognized the importance of the contribution of family farming to sustained, sustainable, and integrated agricultural and rural development of the Andean countries and pledged to promote the Guidelines for Family Agriculture.

On gender and equal opportunities. The Andean Council of High Female Authorities and Equal Opportunities – CAAAMI, created in 2009, promotes actively and permanently work in this area, through actions under the Andean Program for Gender Equality and Equal Opportunities, which are aimed primarily at ensuring the

24. Integrated Social Development Plan, Decision 601, Extraordinary Meeting of the Andean Council of Foreign Affairs Ministers, 21 Sep. 2004.
25. The Gini coefficient is a measurement of inequality developed by Italian statistician Conrado Gini. It is used to measure inequality in the income within a country.

expansion of access to decision-making positions, promoting the economic empowerment of Andean citizens, prevention of violence against women, and teen pregnancy.

333. In regards to *labour and employment*, amongst other challenges listed, there is the diminishment of employment uncertainty and instability as a consequence of processes such as productive restructuring and the transformation of the employment market as a result of the current techno-productive revolution.

Other lines of action in this field also consider intensifying the horizontal technical cooperation between the Labour Ministries in the subregion.

334. It is also foreseen to ensure the active participation of the Labour Ministers Advisory Council and of the Andean Entrepreneurial and Labour Consulting Councils in the elaboration of a future employment-fomenting Andean regulation and to promote the participation of the labour and entrepreneurial sectors in the design, execution, and evaluation of the national production reactivation and employment generation policies.

Likewise, in the Lima Declaration adopted at the Fourteenth Meeting of the Advisory Council of Labour Ministers on 19 and 20 November 2012, the implementation of the Andean Employment Network 'Red Ande' was agreed upon, whose purpose is to link labour supply and demand in the Andean regional labour market.

335. Currently, the Andean Network of Employment Offices is being strengthened, the Andean Workplace Security and Health Instrument (Decision 584 and its Regulation Resolution 957) is being implemented, and the Andean Social Security Instrument (Decision 583) is being regulated.

336. Also, in the Declaration made by the VII CADS that took place in Lima, Peru, on 6 July 2011, it is established as a CAN objective to promote full employment, the economic and productive inclusion, and dignified and decent employment. To those effects, as goals to be achieved by 2019, are: to reduce by 10% the sub-employed population, by one-third the unemployment rate, and increase by 50% the coverage provided by social security to the economically active population.

337. In matters of education, amongst the main challenges to be considered is the coverage in education – still lacking – and to tend to the improving of its quality.

To this regard, programmes are being developed and they consider: the improving of educational quality, the promotion of talent and formation in human resources for strategic sectors; the educational inclusion of vulnerable groups; effective campaigns of Integration values education; better training of human capital, special children and refugees in border zones; education in intercultural adjustment, environment, and development; the establishment of common educational indicators and the homologation of degrees.

338. In the CADS Declaration,[26] which took place on 6 July 2011, it was established as a CAN strategy to guarantee the universal education of the population, with quality, equality, and the use of information technologies.

In the said document, it has been set as goals to be accomplished by 2019, the eradication of analphabetism; to achieve the universal coverage in primary and secondary education and to increase by 50% the coverage in initial education; to improve by 50% the performance in Mathematics and reading comprehension; to increase by 80% the

26. Declaration made by the VII Andean Social Development Ministers Council that took place on 6 Jul. 2011.

number of schools with internet connectivity and by 40% the access to higher education of young people in poverty situations.

339. Alternatively, there exist regulations such as Decision 545, which regulate the displacement of Andean migrant workers, respecting – such as it is established in Decision 583 – their rights to Social Security and guaranteeing adequate conditions of Workplace Safety and Health (Decision 584).

340. Likewise, on 2013, the Human Migrations Development Andean Plan was approved, through which it is sought to reinforce the protection of human and labour rights in third countries, as well as perfecting the coordination to facilitate the migratory flow of Andean cities in the intra-community space, according to standing regulations.

341. In this context, in regards to migrations, it is contemplated in the Andean Strategic Agenda as projects of the CAN: To design and implement a joint action strategy to face the impact of the hardening of national and regional migratory policies in the main destination countries of Andean migration; to regulate and implement Decision 545 Labour Migration Andean Instrument, considering the specific conditions of the countries; implement Decision 548 Consular Assistance and Protection, which was regulated in 2013 by Resolution 1546, that seeks to protect the Andean nationals who are in the territory of third countries; to implement the regulation regarding 'Recognition of national identification documents' (Decision 503); to adequate the community regulation to the standing international instruments of human traffic and illicit migrant traffic; to implement cooperation projects to combat the human traffic and illicit migrant traffic.

342. In the subject of *Food Safety* in the CADS Declaration,[27] it has been established as a CAN objective to achieve security and sovereignty on this regard, for which, as goals to be reached progressively by 2019, it has been established: to reduce by 50% child chronic malnutrition; to reduce by half the prevalence of child anaemia; to reduce by 10 percentile points the percentile of overweight and obese population; and to increment by 50% the participation of production of the Andean subregion in the availability of basic foods.

343. In *matters of Social Security*, in 2004, Decision 583 'Andean Social Security Instrument' was approved, through which an Andean-level applicable reference framework is established, based on basic cooperation principles and commitments, applicable to all Social Security regimes. Through this regulation, the community regulation is adapted to the Common Market objective and the current structure of the Social Security systems in the Andean countries.

344. One of the great challenges that exist in this subject is to achieve the broadening of coverage of health services, to the end of achieving better equality and diminish the great existing social gaps. In this regard, it is best to keep in mind that in the CADS Declaration (%) it has been established as a CAN objective to ensure the health of the population with access to quality universal health services.

345. To those effects, as goals to be met by 2019, it has been established: to reduce by at least one-third, child, neonatal and maternal mortality; to increment by 100% the coverage of health services; to reduce the transmission of HIV from mothers to children to less than 2% and the incidence of congenital syphilis to less than 0.5

27. Declaration made by the VII Andean Social Development Ministers Council that took place on 6 Jul. 2011.

cases per 1000 live births; to keep lethality by grave dengue to less than 2%; to reduce by at least one-third the premature mortality by non-transmissible diseases in the 30–70 year age bracket; to reduce by one-third the percentage of teenage pregnancy.

§6. ENVIRONMENT

346. Taking into consideration that because of its geographic location and the presence of the Andean Range it is an area with a great diversity of climates, cultures, ecosystems, and species, the CAN assigns it special relevance to the protection of the environment and the promotion of a development attuned with nature.

347. Bolivia, Ecuador, Colombia, and Peru have amongst their challenges to collaborate and cooperate in regards to the common objectives of conserving and using in a sustainable way the biodiversity, contribute to reducing the risk and impact of natural and anthropogenic phenomena may occur in the subregion, promoting the undergoing of initiatives for the management of water resources, and the definition and implementation of work plans to face the effects of climate change.

348. In this context, 'One of the greatest challenges for the Member Countries of the Andean Community is to level economic growth with social development, making sustainable use of the natural resources and minimizing the impact on the environment.'[28]

To these effects, the Andean Strategic Agenda has foreseen to foment the cultural and natural patrimony; to develop the existing strategies for biodiversity and prevention and response to disasters; to establish a network for the coordination and exchange of information between the existing national institutes that deal with the subject of biodiversity; as well as, setting up initiatives for the management of water resources and the definition and implementation of work plans regarding climate change.

It is also scheduled to promote projects for the measurement of the impact of situations that affect the environment of the Andean countries, based on international standards and to strengthen and promote the permanent activity of the Andean Council of Ministers of Environment and sustainable development (Decision 596), the Andean Committee of Environmental Authorities (Decision 435), and the Andean Committee for Disaster Prevention and Care (Decision 529)

In accordance with the aforementioned challenges, the activities of the Environmental Work Group are framed in the development of three main instruments: the Andean strategy for the integrated management of water resources (Decisión 763), the Regional Biodiversity Strategy for the Countries of the Andean Tropic (ERB) (Decisión 523), and the Andean Strategy for the Prevention and Response to Disasters (EAPAD).

Additionally the Andean Environmental Agenda 2012–2016 approved by the Andean Council of Ministers of the Environment and Sustainable Development is also a framework for the area in the issues of biodiversity, climate change, and water.

28. And where do we begin? Priorities of the Andean Community regarding Climate Change (Lima, Peru: General Secretary of the Andean Community, the United Nations Program for the Environment, Regional Office for Latin America and the Caribbean, and the Spanish Agency for International Cooperation, 2007), 37.

349. For the execution of the scheduled activities, the CAN has the backing of several sources of international cooperation, such as the Government of Finland, the Ministry of Environment and Rural and Marine Environments, the Autonomous Body of National Parks of Spain, the World Bank, the Global Environment Fund (GEF) and the Government of Japan, amongst others.

In regards to the ERB, it is established that exotic species constitute one of the main reasons for the loss of biological biodiversity on a global scale and a serious threat to the mega diversity of the Andean region.[29] In this respect the necessity to stimulate, advise, orient, and harmonize the national actions is contemplated, to the end of achieving an efficient regional control system of them based on the close cooperation between the Member Countries.

350. Furthermore, the EAPAD envisions a set of policies and guidelines to achieve a reduction of the risk and impact of natural and manmade disasters in the Andean Subregion to assist in the sustainable development of the Member Countries. To that effect, the institutional strengthening and the establishment of common policies, strategies, programmes, and sub programmes are strived for, as well as the exchange of experiences, the creation of networks, and the improving of mutual cooperation in disaster situations.

351. Also, work is being performed in the formulation and implementation of the following regional projects:

(a) Project for the adaptation to the impact of the accelerated glacial withdrawal in the Tropical Andes (PRAA) (Global Environmental Fund, Government of Japan, World Bank).
(b) Regional Biodiversity Programme in the Amazon region of Member Countries of the Andean Community (BIOCAN) (Government of Finland).
(c) Programme for the conservation and sustainable use of biodiversity associated to the network of ancestral Andean roads (Ministry of Environment and Rural and Marine Environments, the Autonomous Body of National Parks of Spain-AECID).
(d) Project for the Analysis of Earth Crust Dynamics in Member Countries of the Andean Community (Andean Regional Programme AECID/CAN – Ecolaboral Programme COSUDE – CONDESAN.
(e) Program Adaptation to Climate Change in the Andean Region (ACC Programme) – SGCAN – GIZ.

352. In the CADS Declaration,[30] it has been established as a CAN objective in this matter to promote prevent, manage, and reduce the impact of climate change and natural disasters on poverty and high-vulnerability populations.

As such, it has been considered as a goal for 2019 that at least 70% of populations in poverty and high-vulnerability are organized and trained in the prevention of social impact derived from climate change and natural disasters, and to ensure that the public,

29. Regional Biodiversity Strategy for the Countries in the Andean Tropic, Executive Summary, 3.
30. Declaration made by the VII Andean Social Development Ministers Council that took place on 6 Jul. 2011.

private and aware, organized population entities manage the risks of natural disasters and climate change consequences in an articulated manner.

§7. Tourism

353. One of the guiding axes of regional and cross-sector integration is the development of tourism.

The activities of the CAN in tourism are focused on two main tools: (a) the design of a competitiveness and tourism development strategy for the Andean Community, through which Andean tourist attractions are promoted and the quality of the tourist services provided on the multiple destinations and products in the subregion are improved; (b) the construction of the satellite Andean tourist region, to the end of quantifying the economic impact of tourism and defining indicators, which help the sector authorities in the continuing control and evaluation of their policies.

354. The Andean Committee of Tourism Authorities (CAATUR) is the body in charge of defining the action plans and strategic guidelines for the development of the common regulating framework and a responsible and sustainable tourism.

Also, activities leading to the promotion of the development of networks and fairs about Andean tourist attractions on the regional level are ongoing; as well as promoting the 'Andean Tourist Product' to offer, both within and outside the region and under a common identity, the combined tourist attractions of the Member Countries.

In addition, an information system of the market demand and tourism demand that sustains the Andean Observatory of Tourism of the Andean Community (OBATUR) was created. This tool is available to decision-makers, both public and private entity in the following link: http: //www.obatur.org/.

To date, we have been working on the standardization of three components on the tourism offer: accommodation, restaurant services, and tourism resources, in accordance with the Agenda for the Development of Tourism. We have also begun analysing tourism quality systems of the Member Countries with the aim of establishing a work programme for the creation and implementation of tourist quality seal in the field of CAN.

§8. Security

355. In the subject regarding security, the CAN encompasses matters of political, economical, social, and cultural nature, and it is reflected in the policies for the strengthening of democratic institutionalism and government of laws, defence, health, environment, economical development, and the prevention of natural disasters, amongst others.

In this regard, one of the main challenges the CAN faces is the development of an Andean citizen safety strategy that has as a guiding principle the promotion and protection of human rights and the consolidation of democratic institutions. Other challenges in this matter are the fight against corruption, terrorism, illicit arms trafficking, drugs, security, and police and judicial cooperation.

356. In this context it is contemplated, amongst other points, the execution of actions related to the activation of the community coordination mechanisms to put in effect Decision 587 Guidelines of the Andean Common External Security Policy, periodically evaluating its validity and application; the support of national social development promotion in low safety index regions programmes; the execution of the 'Andean Plan for the Prevention, Combating and Eradication of the Illegal Small and Light Arms Trade in all its aspects' (Decision 552); and the effective implementation of the 'Andean Plan to Combat Corruption' (Decision 668).

§9. Culture

357. Article 129° of the Cartagena Accord states that 'the cultural identity and the formation of citizen values for the Andean integration, as well as, the full participation of the inhabitant in the subregional process, constitute social development objectives of the Andean population'. For the accomplishment of said objectives, Article 131° stipulates the undergoing of actions oriented to spread a greater knowledge of the cultural, historical, and geographical patrimony of the subregion, of its economic and social current state and of the Andean integration process.

In this context, the Andean Presidential Council, in its XVIIth Meeting, celebrated in Tarija in June 2007, expressed its belief that:

> it is necessary to develop and deepen the Andean Community integration process, better taking into account the visions and focus of the Member Countries, with the objective of achieving a unity in the diversity on behalf of living in partnership with our people and in harmony with nature.

358. Also, the Andean Community Strategic Agenda, Lima, Peru calls to 'create a human capital for the reflexive analysis of the Andean cultural integration process in its multiple dimensions, under the principle of complementarities of values and approaches', and to work jointly in the 'promotion of Cultural Industries'.

In this regard the challenges in cultural matters are: the execution of actions aimed to promote, systematize, and spread the varied and valuable cultural expressions and manifestations of the Andean countries and to promote the adoption of an Andean regulation for the promotion of cultural industries.

359. So it is that amongst the actions to be performed are: to strengthen the actions of the Technical Committee for the Prevention of the Illicit Traffic of Cultural Goods, through specific projects and joint actions against third parties; to foment new expressions of citizen participation to promote an Andean integration culture; to promote the Cultural Industries under the agreement Andrés Bello, for which the production of audiovisual and phonographic material (catalogues, concerts, and discs) are being promoted through by financing funds, new markets for marketing and the creation of the Network of Andean Cultural MIPYMES; as well as promoting the Andean Programme of Cultural and Natural Patrimony.

360. It is also advisable to keep in mind that in the CADS Declaration[31] (5), it has been established as a CAN objective to strengthen intercultural adaptability and the Andean and the Latin American identity.

To such effects, it has been established as goals for 2019 to uphold the use of 100% of the living native languages; to promote the growth by 50% of the number of tourists originating from Andean and Latin American countries; to increase by 50% the displays of Andean and South American audiovisual goods and cultural products in public and private circuits in the community space; and to increase by 30% the citizen access to patrimonial and cultural goods.

§10. Cooperation

361. In this matter, the Andean Strategic Agenda ratifies as a priority the 'integral integration', which contemplates as one of its challenges the deepening of the cooperation process in line with the national policies that each Andean country has decided to develop.

In this context, the main challenges are: (a) the fomenting of intra-regional cooperation mechanisms for the balanced and joint development of the CAN Member Countries, through the special assignment of resources for the cooperation in service of national asymmetries; (b) to strengthen the coordination mechanisms for cooperation within the Andean Community; and (c) to implement the International Cooperation Agenda agreed upon by the Andean Committee of Heads of International Cooperation Agencies of the Andean Community (CATOCI), authority responsible for the monitoring of subregional cooperation, with the intention of allowing a better and more efficient rational use of the available resources.

362. The General Secretary has been executing projects of a subregional nature with funds originating from international cooperation, which has allowed consolidating association relationships with several international organizations and governments, such as the EU, the World Bank, the Inter-American Development Bank, the Andean Foment Corporation, Spain, Finland, and France.

As such, international cooperation has become an important partner in the design and implementation by Member Countries of regional policies and strategies that aim at the achievement of their objectives.

§11. Energy

363. To date, the activities suffered by the Andean Community's energy is focused primarily on the electrical interconnection.

31. Declaration made by the VII Andean Social Development Ministers Council that took place on 6 Jul. 2011.

§12. Energy Integration

364. The matter of energy integration, in the framework of respect and protection of the environment, currently has special relevance in the Andean subregional integration process.

Andean Strategic Agenda has identified Energy Integration as one of the twelve relevant strategic areas. So far, the experience of the Andean Community has been geared to the rules on power systems interconnection matters of Member Countries , mainly as an initiative on issues of gas, developed by an ad hoc group that has been inactive since 2005.

The AEA and its Implementation Plan broadened the scope for energy integration in the Andean Community, towards establishing as strategic guidelines of the sector as the following:

- Promote the exchange of information and experience in oil and gas cooperation, mining, and hydropower in the subregion within a framework of respect and protection of the environment.
- Strengthening institutions on issues related to energy integration in general and electricity interconnection and natural gas, in particular.
- To promote the subregion's energy security and environmental protection.
- Promote the development and use of renewable energies.
- Facilitate energy integration processes (including electricity exchanges and interconnection of natural gas systems).
- To promote the subregion's energy security, energy supply, and subregional trade.

§13. Electrical Integration

365. The Member Countries, through Decision 536 'General guideline for the subregional interconnection of electric systems and intra-community electricity exchange' and Decision 639 'Incorporation of Bolivia to the general guideline for the subregional interconnection of electric systems and intra-community electricity exchange', established the legal community framework to promote the development of the electrical issue.

366. Under this Decision on March 2003, the electrical interconnection between Colombia and Ecuador was inaugurated, with important benefits for both Member Countries, and in July 2005, Bolivia announced its decision to join the Community rule.

In November 2009, the Decision 720 was given – which establishes a provisional regulation for the electrical exchange between Colombia and Ecuador – the application framework of Decision 536 was suspended for a period of two years and the Member Countries were encouraged to establish a new general framework for the electrical exchange between Member Countries.

On 22 August 2011, Decision 757 was approved that replaced Decision 720, which includes a temporary scheme for electric exchanges between Ecuador and Peru

(Appendix 2), in addition to bilateral transitional arrangements for Colombia and Ecuador (Annex 1).

It is important to mention that these are temporary schemes, because the ultimate goal for the Member Countries of the Andean Community is to have a general framework for subregional interconnection of power systems in which the principles and general rules are established for intra electricity involving all Andean countries.

367. With the Andean Strategic Agenda, the importance of starting actions for the promotion of hydrocarbon, mining, and hydroelectric cooperation is highlighted, within the framework of respect and protection of the environment by the Member Countries, and the definition of new alternative energy sources.

368. Also, it established the need for: the strengthening of the Council of Energy, Electricity, Hydrocarbons, and Mines Ministers and the Andean Committee of Electricity Policing and Regulating Organisms – CANREL; evaluating the importance of promoting the change of the current energy matrix; fomenting renewable energies; facilitating energy integration processes; evaluating international electric energy transactions and supply and long-term strategic planning scenarios; and strengthening the definition of actions to pursue in regards to electrical interconnection alternatives.

369. Finally, the need for initiating actions oriented to continuing with the monitoring of the policies of electrical interconnection and the initiation of studies, which will allow identifying pilot subregional projects that contribute to promoting the energy matrix change and fomenting renewable energies is highlighted.

§14. Institutional Development

370. As part of the activities to be performed regarding the institutional development of the CAN is the adoption of measures to guarantee the abiding of Andean regulations, as well as the design and execution of programmes and projects planning, tracking, evaluating, and monitoring system for the General Secretary of the Andean Community and an information, coordination, and networking programme between the Bodies and Institutions of the Andean Integration System.

It is also foreseen to continue the actions leading to securing the financing required for the development of the programmes and projects of the Andean Strategic Agenda, as well as establishing an efficiency and results evaluation mechanism for the cooperation programmes in the framework of the CAN.

Appendix 1

DECISION 563

Official Codified Text of the Andean Subregional Integration Agreement (Cartagena Agreement)

THE COMMISSION OF THE ANDEAN COMMUNITY,

HAVING SEEN: The Amending Protocol of the Andean Subregional Integration Agreement (Cartagena Agreement of 1997), known as the "Sucre Protocol," adopted in Quito on June 25, 1997;

CONSIDERING: That the Sucre Protocol entered into force on April 14, 2003; and

That article 32 of the Sucre Protocol stipulates that the Andean Community Commission shall adopt, through a Decision, the amended consolidated text of the Andean Subregional Integration Agreement (Cartagena Agreement) that incorporates the amendments introduced by the cited Protocol and that the necessary changes shall be made in the numbering of the articles;

DECIDES:

Article 1.- To approve the codification of the Andean Subregional Integration Agreement, "The Cartagena Agreement," in the terms that appear in the annex to this Decision.

Article 2.- This Decision replaces Decision 406 of June 25, 1997.

Signed in the Quirama Recinto, Antioquia Department, of the Republic of Colombia, on the twenty-fifth of June of two thousand three.

ANDEAN SUBREGIONAL INTEGRATION AGREEMENT "CARTAGENA AGREEMENT"

THE GOVERNMENTS of Bolivia, Colombia, Ecuador, Peru, and Venezuela,

INSPIRED by the Declaration of Bogotá and by the Declaration of the Presidents of America;

RESOLVED to strengthen the union of their peoples and to lay the foundations for advancing toward the formation of an Andean subregional community;

AWARE that integration constitutes a historical, political, economic, social, and cultural mandate for their countries, in order to preserve their sovereignty and independence;

BASED on the principles of equality, justice, peace, solidarity, and democracy;

DETERMINED to attain such goals by creating an integration and cooperation system that will lead to the balanced, harmonious, and shared economic development of their countries;

AGREE, through their duly authorized plenipotentiary representatives, to enter into the following SUBREGIONAL INTEGRATION AGREEMENT:

CHAPTER I
OBJECTIVES AND MECHANISMS

Article 1.- The objectives of this Agreement are to promote the balanced and harmonious development of the Member Countries under equitable conditions, through integration and economic and social cooperation; to accelerate their growth and the rate of creation of employment; and to facilitate their participation in the regional integration process, looking ahead toward the gradual formation of a Latin American Common Market.

This Agreement also seeks to reduce external vulnerability and to improve the positioning of the Member Countries within the international economic context; to strengthen subregional solidarity, and to reduce existing differences in levels of development among the Member Countries.

These objectives are aimed at bringing about an enduring improvement in the standard of living of the subregion´s population.

Article 2.- Balanced and harmonious development shall lead to a fair distribution among the Member Countries of the benefits deriving from integration, so that the existing differences among them are reduced. The results of that process shall be evaluated periodically, bearing in mind, among other elements, its effects on the growth of each country's total exports, the performance of its balance of trade with the subregion, the evolution of its gross domestic product, the creation of new jobs, and capital formation.

Article 3.- The following mechanisms and measures shall be used, among others, to fulfill the objectives of this Agreement:

a) The integration with other economic blocs in the region will be intensified and political, social and economic-trade relations will be established with extra-regional systems.

b) Economic and social policies will be gradually harmonized and national laws with regard to pertinent matters will be aligned;

c) Joint programming will be instituted, subregional industrialization will be intensified, industrial programs will be implemented, and other means of industrial integration will be applied;

d) A more advanced schedule of trade liberalization than the commitments derived from the 1980 Treaty of Montevideo will be instituted;

e) A Common External Tariff will be adopted;

f) Programs will be carried out to accelerate the development of the agricultural and agroindustrial sectors;

g) Resources will be channeled from in and outside the Subregion to finance the investments needed by the integration process;

h) Programs will be conducted in the areas of services and the liberalization of intra-subregional trade in services;

i) Physical integration will be pursued; and

j) Bolivia and Ecuador will receive preferential treatment.

In addition to the mechanisms set out above, the following economic and social cooperation programs and aims shall be carried out in a concerted effort:

a) Programs to promote scientific and technological development;

b) Border integration measures;

c) Programs in the area of tourism;

d) Activities for the use and preservation of natural resources and the environment;

e) Social development programs: and

f) Efforts in the field of social communications.

Article 4.- To carry out this Agreement in the best way possible, Member Countries shall make the necessary efforts to seek adequate solutions to the problems stemming from Bolivia's landlocked condition.

CHAPTER II

ON THE ANDEAN COMMUNITY AND THE ANDEAN INTEGRATION SYSTEM

Article 5.- The "Andean Community" is hereby created, composed of the sovereign States of Bolivia, Colombia, Ecuador, Peru, and Venezuela, and of the bodies and institutions of the Andean Integration System, and is established by this Agreement.

Article 6.- The Andean Integration System is made up of the following bodies and institutions:

- The Andean Presidential Council;
- The Andean Council of Foreign Ministers;
- The Andean Community Commission;
- The Andean Community General Secretariat;
- The Andean Community Court of Justice;
- The Andean Parliament;
- The Business Advisory Council;
- The Labor Advisory Council;
- The Andean Development Corporation;
- The Latin American Reserve Fund;
- The Simón Rodríguez Convention, the Social Conventions that join the Andean Integration System, and those that are created within its framework;
- The Simón Bolívar Andean University;
- The Advisory Councils established by the Commission; and,
- All other bodies and institutions that are created within the framework of Andean subregional integration.

Article 7.- The purpose of the System is to allow for effective coordination among its component bodies and institutions, in order to deepen Andean subregional integration, promote its external influence and consolidate and strengthen actions related to the integration process.

Article 8.- The bodies and institutions of the Andean Integration System are governed by this Agreement and by their respective establishing treaties and amending protocols.

Article 9.- In order to achieve the best possible coordination within the Andean Integration System, the Chairman of the Andean Council of Foreign Ministers will call and chair the Meetings of Representatives of the institutions that comprise the System.

The main tasks of the Meeting shall be:

a) To exchange information about the actions taken by the respective institutions to carry out the Guidelines issued by the Andean Presidential Council;

b) To study the possibility and desirability of arranging, among all or some of the institutions, to carry out coordinated actions that will contribute to the achievement of the objectives of the Andean Integration System; and,

c) To present to the Andean Council of Foreign Ministers meeting in enlarged session, reports about the actions carried out in fulfillment of the Guidelines that have been received.

Article 10.- The Representatives of the institutions comprising the Andean Integration System shall meet in regular session at least once a year and in special session whenever requested to do so by any of the member institutions, at the site agreed upon before the meeting is called.

The Andean Community General Secretariat shall act as the Secretariat for the Meeting.

Section A - On The Andean Presidential Council

Article 11.- The Andean Presidential Council is the highest-level body of the Andean Integration System and is made up of the Heads of State of the Member Countries of the Cartagena Agreement. It issues Guidelines on the different spheres of Andean subregional integration, which are carried out by the System bodies and institutions determined by the Council, in keeping with the responsibilities and mechanisms established in their respective Treaties or establishing Agreements.

The bodies and institutions of the System shall guide their policies in the way directed by the Guidelines issued by the Andean Presidential Council.

Article 12.- It is the Andean Presidential Council's responsibility:

a) To define Andean subregional integration policy;

b) To guide and promote action on matters of interest to the Subregion as a whole, as well as on those related to the coordination among the bodies and institutions of the Andean Integration System;

c) To evaluate the development and results of the Andean subregional integration process;

d) To consider and issue opinions about reports, initiatives, and recommendations that are submitted by the bodies and institutions of the Andean Integration System; and

e) To study all issues and matters concerning the course of Andean subregional integration and its external projection.

Article 13.- The Andean Presidential Council shall meet regularly once a year, preferably in the country that chairs it. In this meeting, it shall review the actions taken by the bodies and institutions of the Andean Integration System, as well as their projects, programs, and suggestions. The members of the Andean Council of Foreign Ministers and of the Commission, and representatives of the System bodies and institutions, may attend the meetings of the Andean Presidential Council as observers.

The Andean Presidential Council may meet in special session whenever it considers this advisable, at the place agreed upon before the meeting is called.

Article 14.- The Andean Presidential Council shall have a Chairman who shall be the Andean Community's top political representative, and who shall hold office for a period of one calendar year. That position shall be filled, successively and in alphabetical order, by each of the Member Countries.

The responsibilities of the Chairman of the Andean Presidential Council shall be:

a) To convene and chair the regular and special meetings of the Council;

b) To represent the Council and the Andean Community;

c) To ensure that the Guidelines issued by the Council are carried out by the other bodies and institutions of the Andean Integration System; and,

d) To carry out all tasks requested by the Council.

Section B - On the Andean Council of Foreign Ministers

Article 15.- The Andean Council of Foreign Ministers is comprised of the Ministers of Foreign Affairs of the Member Countries of the Cartagena Agreement.

Article 16.- The responsibilities of the Andean Council of Foreign Ministers are:

a) To formulate the Member Countries´ foreign policy on matters of subregional interest, as well as to orient and coordinate the external efforts of the different bodies and institutions of the Andean Integration System;

b) To formulate, carry out, and evaluate general Andean subregional integration policy, in coordination with the Commission;

c) To carry out the Guidelines given to it by the Andean Presidential Council and to ensure the execution of those that are intended for the other bodies and institutions of the Andean Integration System;

d) To sign Conventions and Agreements with third countries or groups of countries or with international organizations in regard to global foreign policy and cooperation issues;

e) To coordinate, within its sphere of responsibility, the joint position of the Member Countries in international forums and negotiations;

f) To represent the Andean Community, within the sphere of its competence, in matters and acts of common interest, according to the rules and objectives of the Agreement;

g) To recommend or adopt measures within its area of responsibility that will ensure the accomplishment of the purposes and objectives of the Cartagena Agreement;

h) To ensure harmonious compliance with the obligations set out in this Agreement and in the 1980Treaty of Montevideo;

i) To approve and modify its own regulations;

j) To approve the General Secretariat's Regulations and all amendments thereto at the proposal of the Commission;

k) To hear and resolve, within its area of responsibility, all other matters of common interest.

Article 17.- The Andean Council of Foreign Ministers shall express itself through Declarations and Decisions adopted by consensus. The latter shall be a part of Andean Community Law.

Article 18.- The Andean Council of Foreign Ministers shall meet in regular session twice a year, preferably in the country that chairs the Council. It may also meet in special session, when deemed advisable, at the request of any of its members, in the place agreed upon before the meeting is convened.

Article 19.- The Andean Council of Foreign Ministers shall be headed by the Foreign Minister of the country that chairs the Andean Presidential Council, who shall hold office for a period of one calendar year.

The coordination work corresponding to the Chairman of this Council shall be performed by the Foreign Ministry of the country whose Head of State chairs the

Andean Presidential Council, acting as the Pro Tempore Secretariat of both bodies and with the technical support of the Andean Community General Secretariat.

Article 20.- The Andean Council of Foreign Ministers shall meet in enlarged session with the delegation representatives to the Commission at least once a year and, at the level of alternative representatives, whenever it considers it necessary, in order to discuss matters related to the Cartagena Agreement that are of interest to both bodies, such as:

a) To prepare the meetings of the Andean Presidential Council;

b) To choose and, when suitable, remove the General Secretary of the Andean Community;

c) To propose to the Andean Presidential Council any amendments to this Agreement;

d) To evaluate the performance of the General Secretariat;

e) To consider the initiatives and proposals submitted for its consideration by the Member Countries or the General Secretariat; and,

f) Any other issues that both bodies decide to address jointly by common agreement.

Section C - The Andean Community Commission

Article 21.- The Andean Community Commission shall be comprised of a plenipotentiary representative from each Member Country's government, which shall accredit a representative and an alternate representative.

The Commission shall express its will through Decisions.

Article 22.- It is the responsibility of the Andean Community Commission:

a) To formulate, carry out, and evaluate Andean subregional integration policy in the area of trade and investment and, when in order, in coordination with the Andean Council of Foreign Ministers;

b) To take the necessary measures to accomplish the objectives of the Cartagena Agreement and to implement the Guidelines laid down by the Andean Presidential Council;

c) To coordinate, within its sphere of responsibility, the joint position of the Member Countries in international forums and negotiations;

d) To ensure harmonious compliance with the obligations set out in this Agreement and in the 1980 Treaty of Montevideo;

e) To approve and amend its own regulations;

f) To approve, reject or amend the proposals submitted to it by the Member Countries, individually or collectively, or by the General Secretariat;

g) To maintain ongoing relations with the bodies and institutions comprising the Andean Integration System, in order to boost the coordination of programs and measures aimed at accomplishing its common objectives;

h) To represent the Andean Community, within the sphere of its responsibilities, in matters and acts of common interest, in keeping with the rules and objectives of this Agreement;

i) To approve the annual budgets and evaluate the budgetary performance of the General Secretariat and the Andean Community Court of Justice, and to set the contributions to be paid by each of the Member Countries; and,

j) To submit the proposed Regulations of the General Secretariat for consideration by the Andean Council of Foreign Ministers.

In fulfilling its responsibilities, the Commission shall give special consideration to Bolivia and Ecuador's situation in terms of the objectives of this Agreement, the preferential treatment provided in their favor, and Bolivia's landlocked status.

Article 23.- The Commission shall have a Chairman, who shall hold office for one calendar year. That office shall be filled by the representative of the country that is currently chairing the Andean Presidential Council.

Article 24.- The Commission shall meet on a regular basis three times a year and in special session whenever such a meeting is called by its Chairman at the request of any of the Member Countries or the General Secretariat.

Its sessions shall be held at the headquarters of the General Secretariat, but they may also take place elsewhere. The Commission shall meet with the presence of an absolute majority of the Member Countries.

Attendance at Commission meetings is obligatory and failure to attend shall be considered an abstention.

Article 25.- At the request of one or more of the Member Countries or of the General Secretariat, the Commission's Chairman shall summon the Commission to meet as an Enlarged Commission, in order to address sector issues, consider regulations for coordinating the development plans and harmonizing the economic policies of the Member Countries, and hear and resolve all other matters of common interest.

The meetings shall be presided over by the Commission Chairman and shall be jointly comprised of the representatives to the Commission and the Ministers or Secretaries of State of the respective area. Each country is entitled to cast one vote in order to approve Decisions that will become a part of Andean Community Law.

Article 26.- The Commission shall adopt its Decisions by affirmative vote of the absolute majority of the Member Countries. The exceptions to this general rule are:

a) The matters included in Annex 1 to this Agreement, in which case the Commission shall adopt its Decisions by the affirmative vote of the Member Countries with no negative votes being cast.

The Commission may add new matters to that Annex through the affirmative vote of the absolute majority of the Member Countries;

b) For the cases listed in Annex II, General Secretariat proposals shall be approved with the affirmative vote of the absolute majority of the Member Countries, provided that no negative vote is cast. Any proposal that receives the affirmative votes of the absolute majority of the Member Countries, but also a negative vote, shall be returned to the General Secretariat for consideration of the grounds for that negative vote. Within a period of no less than two months or more than six, the General Secretariat shall present the proposal once again for consideration by the Commission, including any modifications it deems appropriate. The amended proposal shall be considered approved if it receives the affirmative vote of the absolute majority of the Member Countries, with no negative vote. In this case, the vote of the country that had dissented previously shall not be counted as a negative vote; and

c) Industrial Development Programs and Projects shall be approved with the affirmative vote of the absolute majority of the Member Countries, provided that no negative vote is cast.

Article 27.- The General Secretariat or the Member Countries shall present their proposals at least fifteen days prior to the corresponding meeting of the Andean Council of Foreign Ministers or of the Commission. Only in duly justified exceptional cases and in accordance with Andean Community Law may the required deadlines be waived, provided that both the proponent and the other Member Countries agree to this.

Proposals that receive the affirmative vote of the absolute majority of the Member Countries, but also a negative vote, shall be returned to the proponent for consideration of the grounds that gave rise to that negative vote.

Within a period of no less than one month or more than three, the proponent shall once again present the proposal for consideration by the corresponding body, incorporating any modifications it considers appropriate. In that case, the amended proposal shall be considered approved if receives the affirmative vote of the absolute majority of the Member Countries.

Article 28.- Any Member Country that falls behind more than four quarters in the payment of its contributions to the General Secretariat or to the Andean Community Court of Justice may not exercise its right to vote in the Commission until it resolves that situation.

In such cases, the quorum for attendance and voting shall be computed according to the number of contributing countries.

Section D - The Andean Community General Secretariat

Article 29.- The General Secretariat is the executive body of the Andean Community and, as such, acts solely in accordance with the interests of the Subregion. The General Secretariat shall give technical support, when appropriate, to the other bodies and institutions of the Andean Integration System.

The General Secretariat shall be headed by the General Secretary. In performing his duties, the General Secretary shall rely on the Directors General, in accordance with the respective regulations. The General Secretary shall also enjoy the services of any technical and administrative staff needed to accomplish his duties. The General Secretariat shall express itself through Resolutions.

Article 30.- The Andean Community General Secretariat's responsibilities are:

a) To ensure the application of this Agreement and compliance with the provisions that comprise Andean Community Law;

b) To carry out the tasks assigned to it by the Andean Council of Foreign Ministers and the Commission;

c) To formulate and put forward draft Decisions to the Andean Council of Foreign Ministers and the Commission, in accordance with their respective spheres of responsibility, and initiatives and suggestions to the enlarged meeting of the Andean Council of Foreign Ministers, aimed at facilitating or hastening the fulfillment of this Agreement, so that its objectives may be achieved within the shortest possible time frame;

d) To conduct studies and propose the necessary measures for applying the special treatments in benefit of Bolivia and Ecuador and, in general, those regarding the participation of the two countries in this Agreement;

e) To study and report annually to the Andean Council of Foreign Ministers and the Commission, on the results of the application of this Agreement and the achievement of its objectives, paying special attention to the fulfillment of the principle of fair distribution of the benefits of integration, and to propose pertinent corrective measures;

f) To perform the technical studies and coordination entrusted to it by other bodies of the Andean Integration System, together with any others it considers necessary;

g) To maintain permanent working relations with the Member Countries, in coordination with the national integration body appointed by each country for that purpose;

h) To draw up its annual working program, in which it shall give preference to the tasks assigned to it by other System bodies;

i) To promote periodic meetings of the national organizations responsible for economic policy formulation or execution and, particularly, those charged with economic planning;

j) To maintain working relations with the executive bodies of other regional integration and cooperation organizations, in order to strengthen their relationship and reciprocal cooperation;

k) To keep the records of the enlarged meetings of the Andean Council of Foreign Ministers and of the Commission, and to draw up a tentative agenda of their meetings, in coordination with the chairmen of those bodies;

l) To be the depository for the records of the meetings and other documents of Andean Integration System bodies and to certify their authenticity;

m) To publish the Official Gazette of the Cartagena Agreement;

n) To act as Secretariat for the Meeting of Representatives of the institutions that comprise the Andean Integration System; and,

ñ) To carry out all other responsibilities expressly assigned to it by Andean Community Law.

Article 31.- The General Secretariat shall operate on a permanent basis and its headquarters shall be located in the city of Lima, Peru.

Article 32.- The General Secretariat shall be headed by a Secretary General who shall be chosen by consensus of the Andean Council of Foreign Ministers for a five-year term of office and may be reelected a single time.

The Secretary General shall be a person with broad representation and acknowledged prestige, and must be a national of one of the Member Countries. He shall act only in the interests of the Subregion as a whole.

The Secretary General may not carry out any other activity during his term of office; nor shall he seek or accept instructions from any government, national institution or international organization.

If the office falls vacant, the Andean Council of Foreign Ministers, meeting in enlarged session, shall immediately proceed to appoint a new Secretary General by consensus. Until that time, the Director-General with the most seniority shall temporarily head the General Secretariat.

Article 33.- The Secretary General may be removed from office by consensus, at the request of a Member Country, only if, in the exercise of his duties, he commits the gross negligence foreseen in the General Secretariat Regulations.

Article 34.- The responsibilities of the Andean Community Secretary General are:

a) To act as the General Secretariat's legal representative;

b) To propose initiatives in regard to the General Secretariat Regulations to the Commission or to the Andean Council of Foreign Ministers;

c) To hire and dismiss technical and administrative staff, in accordance with the General Secretariat Regulations;

d) To participate with the right to be heard in the sessions of the Andean Council of Foreign Ministers and the Commission and in their respective enlarged meetings, and, when invited to do so, in the meetings of other System bodies;

e) To present the draft annual budget to the Commission for its approval; and,

f) To present an annual report of the General Secretariat's activities to the Andean Council of Foreign Ministers meeting in enlarged session.

Article 35.- The Secretary General, in consultation with the Member Countries and in keeping with the General Secretariat's functional and organic structure, shall appoint the Directors-General. These persons shall be top-level professionals, appointed strictly in accordance with their academic background, suitability, reputation, and experience, and they shall each be responsible for a specific technical area.

The Directors-General shall be nationals of Member Countries and the Secretary General shall seek to ensure balanced subregional geographic distribution in their appointment. The appointment and dismissal of the Directors-General shall be governed by the General Secretariat Regulations.

Article 36.- In proceedings where the interests of two or more Member Countries are in dispute, the Secretary General shall enjoy the technical assistance of special experts, whose appointment and method of participation shall be determined according to the General Secretariat Regulations.

Article 37.- The Secretary General, when hiring technical and administrative staff, who may be of any nationality, shall bear in mind strictly the ability, competence, and reputation of the candidates and shall seek to ensure balanced subregional geographic distribution, provided that this is compatible with the preceding criteria.

Personnel shall be appointed and dismissed according to the criteria and grounds established in the General Secretariat Regulations, without prejudice to what the establishing Treaty of the Court of Justice and its amending protocols provide for.

Article 38.- The staff of the General Secretariat shall refrain from taking any action that may be incompatible with the nature of their duties and shall neither seek nor accept instructions from any Government, national institution or international organization.

Article 39.- In the case of proceedings that should conclude with the adoption of a Resolution or Opinion, public or private individuals or legal entities from the Member Countries shall cooperate in such investigations as the General Secretariat may make in carrying out its duties and, in this sense, shall supply any information they are requested for this purpose.

The General Secretariat shall keep any documents and information furnished strictly confidential, in accordance with the rules governing those matters.

Section E - On the Andean Community Court of Justice

Article 40.- The Court of Justice is the judicial authority of the Andean Community.

Article 41.- The Andean Community Court of Justice is governed by its establishing Treaty and its amending protocols and this Agreement.

The Court has its headquarters in the city of Quito, Ecuador.

Section F - On The Andean Parliament

Article 42.- The Andean Parliament is the System's deliberating body. It has a community nature, represents the peoples of the Andean Community and shall be made up of representatives chosen by universal and direct suffrage, according to the procedure that is adopted through an Additional Protocol that shall include adequate criteria for national representation.

Until the Additional Protocol instituting direct elections is signed, the Andean Parliament shall be comprised of representatives of the National Congresses, in accordance with their internal regulations and the General Regulations of the Andean Parliament.

The headquarters of the Andean Parliament shall be in the city of Bogotá, Colombia.

Article 43.- The Andean Parliament's responsibilities are:

a) To participate in the promotion and guidance of the Andean Subregional integration process, with a view to consolidating Latin American integration;

b) To examine the progress of the Andean subregional integration process and the fulfillment of its objectives, requesting periodic information from the System bodies and institutions for that purpose;

c) To formulate recommendations regarding the annual draft budgets of the System bodies and institutions that are financed through the direct contributions of the Member Countries;

d) To suggest to the System bodies and institutions actions or decisions, whose goal or effect is the adoption of modifications, adjustments, or new general guidelines in relation to the programmed objectives and institutional structure of the System;

e) To participate in the law-making process by suggesting to the System bodies draft provisions on subjects of common interest, for incorporation in Andean Community Law;

f) To promote the harmonization of Member Country legislation; and,

g) To promote cooperative and coordinated relations with Member Country Parliaments, System bodies and institutions, and third country parliamentary integration or cooperation bodies.

Section G - On the Advisory Institutions

Article 44.- The Business Advisory Council and the Labor Advisory Council are the consultative institutions of the Andean Integration System. They are comprised of high-level delegates, who shall be directly elected by the representative organizations in the business and labor sectors of each of the Member Countries, according to their respective regulations, and officially accredited by them.

The responsibilities of the Advisory Councils shall be to express their opinions to the Andean Council of Foreign Ministers, the Commission or the General Secretariat, at the request of these bodies or on their own initiative, with regard to programs or activities of the Andean subregional integration process that are of interest to their respective sectors. They can also be summoned to meetings of working groups and of government experts involved in preparing draft Decisions, and may participate in meetings of the Commission with the right to take part in the discussions.

Section H - On the Financial Institutions

Article 45.- The Andean Development Corporation and the Latin American Reserve Fund are the System's financial institutions and their purpose is to promote the Andean subregional integration process.

Article 46.- The General Secretariat and the executive bodies of the Andean Development Corporation and the Latin American Reserve Fund shall maintain working relations for the purpose of coordinating activities adequately and, thereby, facilitating the achievement of the objectives of this Agreement.

Section I - On Dispute Settlement

Article 47.- The settlement of any disputes that may arise as a result of the application of Andean Community Law shall abide by the provisions of the Treaty establishing the Court of Justice.

Section J - On the International Legal Capacity and the Privileges and Immunities

Article 48.- The Andean Community is a subregional organization with an international legal capacity or status.

Article 49.- The General Secretariat, the Court of Justice, the Andean Parliament, the Andean Development Corporation, the Latin American Reserve Fund, and the Social Conventions that are part of the System shall enjoy, within the territory of each of the Member Countries, the privileges and immunities required for the fulfillment of their objectives. Their representatives and international staff shall, likewise, be given the privileges and immunities required to carry out their duties in relation to this agreement with independence. Their premises are inviolable and their goods and property are immune to all judicial proceedings, unless expressly waived. Nevertheless, such a waiver shall not apply to any judicial measures of execution.

CHAPTER III
FOREIGN RELATIONS

Article 50.- The Andean Council of Foreign Ministers shall formulate the Common Foreign Policy on matters that are of interest to the subregion. To that end, it shall coordinate joint political positions that will enable the Community to participate effectively in international political forums and organizations.

Article 51.- The Andean Council of Foreign Ministers and the Andean Community Commission shall define and undertake to implement a community strategy aimed at deepening integration with other economic blocs in the region and establishing political, social and economic-trade relations with other groups outside the region.

Article 52.- In order to accomplish the objective stated in this Chapter, the Andean Council of Foreign Ministers and the Andean Community Commission shall take the following measures, among others:

a) Strengthen community participation in international, multilateral, hemispheric and regional economic and trade forums;

b) Coordinate joint negotiations of the Andean Community with other integration processes or with third countries or groups of countries; and

c) Entrust the General Secretariat to perform research, studies and activities that will make it possible to achieve the objective and carry out the measures provided for in this Chapter.

CHAPTER IV
HARMONIZATION OF ECONOMIC POLICIES AND COORDINATION OF DEVELOPMENT PLANS

Article 53.- The Member Countries shall progressively adopt a strategy to achieve the subregional development objectives envisaged in this Agreement.

Article 54.- The Member Countries shall coordinate their development plans in specific sectors and shall gradually harmonize their economic and social policies, with a view to achieving the integrated development of the area through planned actions.

This process shall be carried out simultaneously and in coordination with the creation of the subregional market, by means of the following mechanisms, among others:

a) Industrial Development Programs;

b) Agricultural and Agroindustrial Development Programs;

c) Physical Infrastructure Development Programs;

d) Intra-subregional Programs for the Liberalization of Services;

e) Harmonization of foreign exchange, monetary, financial, and fiscal policies, including the treatment of subregional or foreign capital;

f) A common trade policy in relation to third countries; and

g) Harmonization of planning methods and techniques.

Article 55.- The Andean Community shall have a common system for the treatment of foreign capital and on trademarks, patents, licenses, and royalties, among other things.

Article 56.- The Andean Community shall have a uniform regime that Andean multinational enterprises must abide by.

Article 57.- The Commission, at the General Secretariat's proposal, shall establish the necessary permanent procedures and mechanisms for achieving the coordination and harmonization referred to in Article 54.

Article 58.- The Commission, at the General Secretariat's proposal and taking into account the progress and needs of the subregional integration process, as well as the balanced compliance with the mechanisms of the Agreement, shall approve provisions and define timeframes for the progressive harmonization of economic legislation and the instruments and mechanisms for regulating and promoting the Member Countries´ foreign trade that affect the mechanisms provided for in this Agreement for the creation of the subregional market.

Article 59.- The Member Countries shall provide in their national development plans and in the formulation of their economic policies for the necessary measures to ensure compliance with the preceding Articles.

CHAPTER V
INDUSTRIAL DEVELOPMENT PROGRAMS

Article 60.- The Member Countries bind themselves to promote a joint industrial development process in order to attain the following objectives, among others:

a) Expansion, specialization, diversification, and promotion of industrial activity;

b) Profitable use of economies of scale;

c) Optimum utilization of the resources available in the area, particularly by industrializing the natural resources;

d) Improvement in productivity;

e) Closer relations, interlinkage and complementarity among the sub region's industrial enterprises;

f) Equitable distribution of benefits; and

g) Better international participation by subregional industry.

Article 61.- For purposes of the previous Article, the following shall constitute modes of industrial integration:

a) Industrial Integration Programs;

b) Industrial Complementarity Agreements; and

c) Industrial Integration Projects.

Section A - On Industrial Integration Programs

Article 62.- The Commission, at the General Secretariat's proposal, shall adopt Industrial Integration Programs, preferably to promote new industrial production lines that are sectoral or intersectoral in scope, and in which at least four Member Countries shall participate.

The programs shall include clauses dealing with:

a) Specific targets;

b) The determination of what products the Program will target;

c) The siting of production facilities in the countries of the subregion whenever the characteristics of the sector or sectors involved so require it, in which case, they shall include provisions on the commitment not to encourage such production in countries that are not favored by the allocation;

d) A Trade Liberalization Program that may provide for different rates of implementation by country and by product;

e) A Common External Tariff;

f) Coordination of new subregion-wide investments and measures to ensure their financing;

g) Harmonization of policies on aspects that affect the Program directly;

h) Complementary measures that may foster greater industrial linkages and facilitate the fulfillment of Program goals; and

i) The timeframes during which the rights and obligations arising from the Program shall be maintained in the event the Agreement is denounced.

Article 63.- A country that is not participating in an Industrial Integration Program may request its incorporation at any time, in which case the Commission shall approve the conditions for that incorporation, through the voting system provided for in Article 26 b). Any negotiations that may have been carried out between the participating countries and the non-participant should be considered in the respective proposals.

Section B - On the Industrial Complementarity Agreements

Article 64.- The aim of Industrial Complementarity Agreements shall be to promote industrial specialization among the Member Countries. Such Agreements may be entered into and carried out by two or more Countries and must be approved by the Commission.

For the purposes of the preceding paragraph, the Agreements may include measures such as the distribution of production, joint production, subcontracting of productive capacities, marketing agreements, and joint foreign trade operations, as well as any other measures that may facilitate closer coordination of the production processes and entrepreneurial activity.

Industrial Complementarity Agreements shall be temporary in nature, and in addition to the determination of target products and of the expiration date of the rights and obligations of the participating Member Countries, may include special measures concerning tariff treatment, trade regulation, and the establishment of preferential margins that are not applicable to non-participant countries, provided that such measures represent equal or better conditions than those existing for reciprocal trade. In that case, the duties applicable to third countries shall be determined.

Article 65.- Countries that are not participating in the Complementarity Agreements may request their incorporation at any time, in which case the participating countries shall approve the conditions for that incorporation, which shall be made known to the Commission.

Section C - On Industrial Integration Projects

Article 66.- The Commission shall approve Industrial Integration Projects at the proposal of the General Secretariat. These projects shall be carried out for specific products or product families --preferably new ones--, through policies of collective cooperation and all of the Member Countries shall be involved.

The following measures, among others, shall be taken for the execution of these Projects:

a) Feasibility and design studies will be prepared;

b) Equipment, technical assistance, technology, and other goods and services, preferably of subregional origin, will be supplied;

c) The support of the Andean Development Corporation will be obtained, in the form of either financing or equity investment; and

d) Joint arrangements and negotiations will be carried out with international entrepreneurs and government agencies to obtain foreign funding or the transfer of technology.

Industrial Integration Projects shall include clauses that deal with the siting of production facilities in the Member Countries whenever the characteristics of the corresponding sector or sectors require it and may include clauses to facilitate the access of products to the subregional market.

In the case of specific projects that are sited in Bolivia or Ecuador, the Commission shall establish temporary and exclusive tariff treatment to improve the terms of access by those products to the subregional market. If products that are not produced in the Subregion are included in this category, the terms of access shall provide for exceptions to the principle of irrevocability stipulated in the first paragraph of Article 76.

Section D - Other Provisions

Article 67.- In applying the modes of industrial integration, the Commission and the General Secretariat shall bear in mind the situation and requirements of small and medium-sized industry, particularly those concerning the following aspects:

a) The installed capacity of existing enterprises;

b) Financial and technical needs for the installation, expansion, modernization, or conversion of production facilities;

c) The prospects for setting up joint marketing and technological research systems and other forms of cooperation among similar enterprises; and

d) Labor training requirements.

Article 68.- Industrial integration methods may provide for industrial streamlining efforts aimed at making the most of the factors of production and reaching higher levels of productivity and efficiency.

Article 69.- The General Secretariat may carry out or promote cooperation efforts, including those aimed at industrial streamlining and modernization in benefit of any activity in the sector, particularly of small and medium-sized subregional industry, for the purpose of contributing to the industrial development of the Member Countries. Priority shall be given to carrying out these actions in Bolivia and Ecuador.

Article 70.- The General Secretariat, whenever it deems it advisable and, in any case, in the course of its periodic evaluations, shall propose to the Commission the measures it considers essential to ensure the equitable participation of the Member Countries in the modes of industrial integration that are covered in this Chapter, their execution, and the attainment of their aims.

Article 71.- It shall be the responsibility of the Commission and of the General Secretariat to coordinate appropriately with the Andean Development Corporation, and to arrange for the assistance of any other national or international institutions whose technical and financial contribution it considers desirable for:

a) Facilitating policy coordination and joint investment programming;

b) Channeling a growing volume of funds to resolve problems created for Member Countries by the industrial integration process;

c) Promoting the financing of investment projects that arise from the execution of the different modes of industrial integration; and

d) Expanding, modernizing, or converting industrial production facilities that may be adversely affected by trade liberalization.

CHAPTER VI
LIBERALIZATION PROGRAM

Article 72.- The purpose of the Liberalization Program for goods is to eliminate duties and restrictions of all kinds levied on the importation of products originating in the territory of any Member Country.

Article 73.- "Duties" are understood to be the customs duties and any other charges with equivalent effects, whether of a fiscal, monetary or foreign exchange nature, that may affect imports. Not included in this concept are analogous assessments and surcharges that correspond to the approximate cost of the services rendered.

"Restrictions of all kinds" are understood to mean any administrative, financial, or foreign exchange measure whereby a Member Country, through a unilateral decision, obstructs or hinders imports. Not included in this concept are the adoption and enforcement of measures to:

a) Protect public morals;

b) Implement laws and regulations on security;

c) Regulate the import or export of weapons, ammunition, and other war materials, and, under special circumstances, all other military articles, provided that this does not interfere with the provisions of treaties in force between Member Countries relating to the freedom of unrestricted transit;

d) Protect the life and health of human beings, animals, and plants;

e) Import and export metallic gold and silver;

f) Protect national treasures with an artistic, historical, or archaeological value; and

g) Export, use and consume nuclear materials, radioactive products, or any other material that may be employed for the development and utilization of nuclear energy.

Article 74.- For the purposes of the previous articles, the General Secretariat, on its own initiative or at the request of a party, shall determine, when necessary, whether a measure adopted unilaterally by a Member Country constitutes a "duty" or "restriction."

Article 75.- Products originating in a Member Country shall enjoy, in the territory of another Member Country, treatment that is no less favorable than that accorded to similar domestic products, insofar as taxes, assessments and other domestic duties are concerned.

Article 76.- The Liberalization Program shall be automatic and irrevocable and shall cover the entire product universe, save for the provisions regarding exceptions that are established in this Agreement, so that a total liberalization is achieved within the timeframes and by the methods referred to in this Agreement.

This Program shall apply, in its various forms, to:

a) Products that are targeted by Industrial Integration Programs;

b) Products that are included in the Common List referred to in Article 4 of the 1960 Montevideo Treaty;

c) Products on the corresponding list that are not produced in any of the subregion's countries; and

d) Products that are not covered in the above-cited sections.

Article 77.- Member Countries shall refrain from levying customs duties and introducing restrictions of any kind on the importation of goods that originated in the subregion.

Article 78.- Member Countries shall seek to jointly reach partial-scope trade agreements, economic complementarity agreements, agricultural agreements, and trade promotion agreements, with the other Latin American countries in sectors where this is feasible, according to the provisions of Article 86 of this Agreement and of the 1980 Montevideo Treaty.

CHAPTER VII
INTRA-SUBREGIONAL TRADE IN SERVICES

Article 79.- The Andean Community Commission, at the proposal of the General Secretariat, shall approve a general framework of principles and provisions for liberalizing the intra-subregional trade in services.

Article 80.- The general framework provided for in the previous article shall be applied to the trade in services provided in the following ways:

a) From the territory of one Member Country to the territory of another Member Country;

b) Within the territory of a Member Country to a consumer from another Member Country;

c) Through the commercial presence of service enterprises of one Member Country in the territory of another Member Country; and,

d) By individuals from one Member Country in the territory of another Member Country.

CHAPTER VIII
COMMON EXTERNAL TARIFF

Article 81.- The Member Countries commit themselves to put a Common External Tariff into effect within the timeframes and according to the modes the Commission may establish.

Article 82.- The Commission, at the General Secretariat's proposal, shall approve the Common External Tariff, which must provide for adequate levels of protection for subregional products, considering the Agreement objective of gradually harmonizing the different economic policies of the Member Countries.

On the date indicated by the Commission, Colombia, Peru, and Venezuela shall begin the process of aligning the customs duties that are applicable under their national tariff schedules to the importation of products that did not originate in the subregion, with the Common External Tariff in an annual, automatic, and linear way.

Article 83.- The stipulations of Article 82 notwithstanding, the following provisions shall be applied:

a) With respect to products that are targeted by Industrial Integration Programs, the rules established by those Programs regarding the Common External Tariff shall govern; and with respect to products that are targeted by Industrial Integration Projects, the Commission, whenever appropriate, may specify, when approving the respective Decision, the levels of customs duties that shall apply to third countries and the corresponding terms; and

b) Whenever, in fulfilling the Liberalization Program, a product is freed from customs duties and other restrictions, it shall be subject to the full and simultaneous application of the customs duties established in the Minimum Common External Tariff or in the Common External Tariff, as the case may be.

In the case of goods that are not produced in the subregion, each country may defer the application of the common customs duties until the General Secretariat verifies that their production has begun in the subregion. Even so, if in the General Secretariat's judgment the new production is insufficient to meet the normal needs of the subregion, it shall propose to the Commission that it adopt the necessary measures to reconcile the need to protect subregional production with that of ensuring a normal supply.

Article 84.- The Commission, at the proposal of the General Secretariat, may modify the common tariff levels to the extent and at the time it deems advisable, in order to:

a) Adjust them to the subregion´s needs; and

b) Provide for the special situations of Bolivia and Ecuador.

Article 85.- The General Secretariat may propose to the Commission the measures it considers essential to ensure normal supply conditions in the subregion.

Any Member Country undergoing temporary supply shortages may report the problem to the General Secretariat, which shall verify the situation within a period commensurate with the urgency of the case. Once the General Secretariat verifies the existence of the problem in question and so informs the country adversely affected, the latter may take steps, such as to temporarily reduce or suspend the External Tariff duties within the necessary limits to correct the disturbance.

In the cases referred to in the previous section, the General Secretariat shall call a special meeting of the Commission, if such is in order, or shall inform it at its following regular meeting regarding the action that has been taken.

Article 86.- The Member Countries commit themselves not to unilaterally alter the customs duties set in the Common External Tariff. They also agree to hold the necessary consultations within the Commission before assuming tariff obligations with countries outside the subregion. The Commission, at the General Secretariat's proposal and through a Decision, shall state its opinion regarding those consultations and shall establish the terms with which tariff commitments must comply.

CHAPTER IX
AGRICULTURAL DEVELOPMENT PROGRAMS

Article 87.- In order to boost common agricultural and agroindustrial development and attain greater subregional food security, the Member Countries shall carry out an Agricultural and Agroindustrial Development Program, harmonize their policies, and coordinate their national plans in this sector, bearing in mind the following objectives, among others:

a) To improve the standard of living of the rural population;

b) To take care to meet the food and nutritional requirements of the population satisfactorily, in order to reduce to the utmost dependence on supplies from outside the subregion;

c) To ensure the timely and adequate supply of the subregional market and protect against the risk of food shortages;

d) To increase the production of staple foods and raise productivity levels;

e) To ensure the complementarity and specialization of the subregion's production, with a view to improving the use of its inputs and increasing the trade in agricultural and agroindustrial products; and

f) To replace the subregion's imports and diversify and increase its exports.

Article 88.- The Commission, at the proposal of the General Secretariat, shall take the following steps, among others, to fulfill the objectives stated in the previous article:

a) Create an Andean and National Food Security Systems;

b) Carry out joint agricultural and agroindustrial development programs, by products or product groups;

c) Implement joint agricultural and agroindustrial technological development programs that include technological research, training, and transfer activities;

d) Promote intra-subregional agricultural and agroindustrial trade and sign agreements to supply agricultural products;

e) Conduct joint programs and activities with regard to agricultural and agroindustrial trade with third countries;

f) Establish and execute common provisions and programs on plant and animal health;

g) Create subregional funding mechanisms for the agricultural and agroindustrial sector;

h) Execute joint programs for the profitable use and conservation of the sector's natural resources; and

i) Implement joint cooperative technological research and transfer programs in areas of common interest to the Member Countries, such as genetics, floriculture, fishing, forestry, and any others the Commission may decide upon in the future.

Article 89.- The Commission and the General Secretariat shall take the necessary measures to step up the agricultural and agroindustrial development of Bolivia and Ecuador, as well as their participation in the enlarged market.

Article 90.- Any Member Country may apply non-discriminatory measures to trade in the products added to the list referred to in Article 92, for the purpose of:

a) Restricting imports to the absolute minimum needed to cover shortages in domestic production; and

b) Bringing the prices of imported products into line with those of the domestic products.

In order to implement such measures, the Member Countries shall, when appropriate, take steps to supply agricultural and agroindustrial food products through existing national agencies.

Article 91.- The country that imposes the measures referred to in the previous article shall immediately notify the General Secretariat, enclosing a report substantiating its action.

These measures shall be applied to Bolivia and Ecuador only in duly qualified cases and after the General Secretariat has confirmed that the damage is due essentially to their imports. The General Secretariat is obliged to express its views within fifteen days after receiving the report and may authorize the measures to be applied.

Any Member Country that considers itself affected by those measures may present its objections to the General Secretariat.

The General Secretariat shall study the case and propose to the Commission the positive measures it deems advisable in the light of the objectives indicated in Article 87.

The Commission shall decide with respect to the restrictions that were applied and the measures that are proposed by the General Secretariat.

Article 92.- The Commission, at the proposal of the General Secretariat, shall decide upon the list of agricultural products to which Articles 90 and 91 may be applied, before December 31, 1970. The Commission may modify that list at the proposal of the General Secretariat.

CHAPTER X
TRADE COMPETITION

Article 93.- the Commission, before December 31, 1971 and at the General Secretariat's proposal, shall adopt the essential provisions to guard against or correct practices that may distort competition within the subregion, such as dumping, improper price manipulations, maneuvers to upset the normal supply of raw materials, and others with a like effect. In this respect, the Commission shall consider the problems that could be created by imposing duties and other restrictions on exports.

It shall be the General Secretariat's responsibility to ensure the application of those provisions to the particular cases that are reported.

Article 94.- The Member Countries may not take corrective measures without prior authorization from the General Secretariat. The Commission shall regulate the procedures for implementing the provisions contained in this Chapter.

CHAPTER XI
SAFEGUARD CLAUSES

Article 95.- Any Member Country that has taken measures to correct an external imbalance may extend those measures, when authorized to do so by the General

Secretariat, temporarily and in a non-discriminatory way, to intra-subregional trade in the products included in the Liberalization Program.

The Member Countries shall seek to ensure that the imposition of restrictions due to an adverse balance of payments situation does not affect trade within the subregion in the products incorporated in the Liberalization Program.

If the situation envisaged in this Article requires an immediate response, the Member Country involved may apply the foreseen measures on an emergency basis. It shall report that action immediately to the General Secretariat, which shall hand down its decision within the following thirty days, either authorizing, modifying, or suspending those measures.

If the application of the measures provided for in this Article continues for a period of over one year, the General Secretariat, on its own initiative or at the request of any of the Member Countries, shall propose to the Commission that negotiations be immediately initiated to seek the removal of those restrictions.

Article 96.- If the implementation of the Agreement's Liberalization Program causes or threatens to cause serious economic damage to a Member Country or to one of its key economic sectors, that country may, with the prior authorization of the General Secretariat, take temporary and non-discriminatory corrective steps. If necessary, the General Secretariat may propose to the Commission that measures of collective cooperation be taken to surmount the problems that have arisen.

The General Secretariat shall periodically study the evolution of the situation to keep the restrictive measures from being imposed any longer than is strictly necessary or to study new formulas for cooperation, if appropriate.

If the damages dealt with in this Article are so serious that they require immediate steps to be taken, the injured Member Country may apply corrective measures temporarily, on an emergency basis, subject to the subsequent decision of the General Secretariat.

Those measures should damage the Liberalization Program as little as possible and, so long as they are implemented unilaterally, may not involve reducing imports of the product or products in question to below the average for the preceding twelve months.

Any Member Country that takes those measures shall immediately report them to the General Secretariat and the latter shall issue its decision within the following thirty days, either authorizing, modifying, or suspending them.

Article 97.- If products that originated in the Subregion are imported in such quantities or conditions as to disrupt a Member Country's production of specific products, that Country may take non-discriminatory and temporary corrective measures, subject to the subsequent decision of the General Secretariat.

A Member Country that takes corrective measures must notify the General Secretariat within no more than sixty days and present a report substantiating their application. The General Secretariat, within sixty days after receiving that report, shall verify the existence of the disruption and the origin of the imports that caused it and shall issue its decision, either suspending, modifying, or authorizing those measures, which may be applied only to the products of the Member Country where the disturbance originated. The corrective measures that are taken shall guarantee the access of a volume of trade amounting to no less than the average for the previous three years.

Article 98.- If a currency devaluation made by one of the Member Countries alters the normal conditions of competition, the country that considers itself to be adversely affected may bring the case before the General Secretariat, which should hand down its decision briefly and summarily. Once the General Secretariat has verified the existence of the disturbance, the country that is adversely affected may take temporary corrective measures so long as the condition exists, while abiding by the General Secretariat's recommendations. In any case, those measures may not involve reducing imports to levels below those that existed prior to the devaluation.

The application of the temporary measures referred to notwithstanding, any Member Country may request the Commission to hand down a final decision on the matter.

The Member Country that devalued its currency may ask the General Secretariat to review the situation at any time, with a view to easing or eliminating the cited corrective measures. The Commission may amend the General Secretariat's decision.

In the situation referred to in this Article, the country which considers itself to be adversely affected may, in presenting the case to the General Secretariat, propose protective measures that are commensurate with the magnitude of the alleged disturbance, accompanied by the technical substantiation of its proposal. The General Secretariat may request any supplementary information it deems advisable.

The General Secretariat shall hand down its brief and summary decision within a period of one month after receiving the request. If it fails to do so within the stipulated period and the requesting country feels that the delay may be harmful to its interests, it may take the initial measures it had proposed; this action shall be immediately reported to the General Secretariat, which shall decide whether the measures that have been applied should be maintained, modified, or suspended.

In communicating its decision, the General Secretariat shall bear in mind, among other criteria, the economic indicators regarding the conditions of trade competition in the subregion adopted in general by the Commission, at the General Secretariat's proposal, the individual characteristics of the Member Countries' foreign exchange systems and any studies which the Monetary and Foreign Exchange Council may have made on the subject.

The General Secretariat shall proceed according to its own criteria until the Commission adopts the system of economic indicators.

Notwithstanding the foregoing, if, during the period between the presentation in question and the General Secretariat's decision, in the opinion of the applicant Member Country, there are background elements which give reasonable grounds to fear that the devaluation may cause immediate harmful effects that may have serious implications for its economy that will require the adoption of protective measures on an emergency basis, it may present the situation to the General Secretariat; the latter, if it finds the request to be well-grounded, shall have a period of seven continuous days in which to authorize suitable measures to be taken. The General Secretariat's final decision regarding the disruption of the normal conditions of competition shall, in any case, determine whether the authorized emergency measures shall be maintained, modified, or suspended.

Measures that are adopted pursuant to this Article may not involve reducing trade to levels below those that existed prior to the devaluation.

The second and third paragraphs of this Article shall be fully applicable to all of these measures.

Article 99.- No safeguard clauses of any kind shall be applied to the importation of products originating in the subregion and included in the Industrial Integration Programs and Projects.

CHAPTER XII
ORIGIN

Article 100.- The Commission, at the General Secretariat's proposal, shall adopt any special provisions that may be needed to determine the origin of goods. Those rules shall constitute a dynamic instrument for the subregion's development and shall be appropriate for helping to attain the Agreement's objectives.

Article 101.- It shall be the General Secretariat's responsibility to establish the specific requirements of origin for the products that require them. If an Industrial Integration Program necessitates the establishment of specific requirements, the General Secretariat shall determine those requirements as the corresponding program is being approved.

The Member Countries may request the General Secretariat to review a specific requirement within a year after its establishment and its decision must be communicated summarily.

If a Member Country so requests, the Commission shall examine the requirements and hand down a final decision within six to twelve months after their establishment by the General Secretariat.

The stipulation of the first paragraph of this article notwithstanding, the General Secretariat may, at any time, either on its own initiative or at the request of a party, establish or modify those requirements in order to adjust them to the subregion's economic and technological progress.

Article 102.- In adopting and establishing the special provisions or specific requirements of origin, as the case may be, the Commission and the General Secretariat shall seek to ensure that they do not hinder Bolivia and Ecuador from taking advantage of the benefits stemming from the Agreement's implementation.

Article 103.- The General Secretariat shall ensure compliance with the rules and requirements of origin in subregional trade. It shall, moreover, propose any measures that are necessary to resolve problems of origin that obstruct the attainment of the objectives of this Agreement.

CHAPTER XIII
PHYSICAL INTEGRATION

Article 104.- The Member Countries shall make a joint effort to improve the use of the physical space and reinforce the infrastructure and services that are needed to advance the subregion's economic integration. This effort shall be made primarily in the fields of energy, transportation, and communications and shall cover the necessary measures for facilitating cross-border traffic between the Member Countries.

To this end, the Member Countries shall seek to establish multinational entities or enterprises whenever possible and desirable to facilitate the execution and administration of those projects.

Article 105.- The Commission, at the General Secretariat's proposal, shall adopt programs in the fields cited to in the preceding Article in order to promote a continuous process aimed at expanding and modernizing the physical infrastructure and the transportation and communications services of the subregion. These programs shall encompass the following, insofar as possible:

a) The identification of specific projects for incorporation in the national development plans and an indication of the order of priority for their execution;

b) The essential measures for financing the necessary preinvestment studies;

c) The technical and financial assistance needs to ensure the execution of the projects; and

d) The joint action to be taken with the Andean Development Corporation and the international lending institutions to ensure that the required financial resources are provided.

Article 106.- The programs referred to in the foregoing Article, as well as the Industrial Integration Programs and Projects, shall include measures of collective cooperation to adequately cover the essential infrastructure required for their execution and shall give special consideration to the situation of Ecuador and Bolivia's territorial and landlocked status.

CHAPTER XIV
FINANCIAL MATTERS

Article 107.- The Member Countries shall take action and coordinate their policies on financial matters and payments to the extent necessary to facilitate the attainment of the Agreement's objectives.

For that purpose, the Commission, at the General Secretariat's proposal, shall provide for the following actions:

a) Recommendations to channel the financial resources through the appropriate bodies in order to meet the subregion's development requirements;

b) Promotion of investments for the Andean integration programs;

c) Financing of trade among the Member Countries and between them and countries outside the subregion;

d) Measures to facilitate the movement of capital within the subregion and particularly the promotion of Andean multinational enterprises;

e) Coordination of positions to strengthen the reciprocal payments and lending mechanisms within the framework of ALADI;

f) Establishment of an Andean financing and payments system that would encompass the Latin American Reserve Fund, a common unit of account, trade credit lines, a subregional clearinghouse, and a system of reciprocal credits;

g) Cooperation and the coordination of positions to handle the Member Countries' external financing problems; and

h) Coordination with the Andean Development Corporation and the Latin American Reserve Fund for the purposes described in the preceding items.

Article 108.- If a Member Country experiences problems with its fiscal revenues as a result of the fulfillment of the Agreement's Liberalization Program, the General Secretariat may propose to the Commission, at the request of the affected country, measures for resolving those difficulties. The General Secretariat shall take into account in its proposals the degrees of relative economic development of the Member Countries.

CHAPTER XV
SPECIAL REGIME FOR BOLIVIA AND ECUADOR

Article 109.- Bolivia and Ecuador shall enjoy a special regime, with a view toward gradually reducing the differences in development that currently exist in the subregion. This system shall enable them to attain more rapid economic growth through effective and immediate participation in the benefits of the area's industrialization and the liberalization of trade.

The bodies of the Agreement shall propose and take the necessary measures to fulfill the aim of this Article, in accordance with its rules.

Section A - On the Harmonization of Economic Policies and the Coordination of Development Plans

Article 110.- In harmonizing the economic and social policies and coordinating the plans referred to in Chapter IV, differential treatments and sufficient incentives shall be established to compensate for Bolivia and Ecuador's structural weaknesses and ensure the mobilization and allocation of the essential resources for attaining the objectives envisaged in the Agreement for their benefit.

Section B - On Industrial Policy

Article 111.- The Industrial Development Programs shall give special consideration to the situations of Bolivia and Ecuador in assigning, on a priority basis, the production for their benefit and the consequent siting of the production facilities in their territories, particularly through their participation in the modes of industrial integration stipulated in Article 58. It shall also provide for the implementation of a program for the comprehensive industrialization of the two countries' natural resources.

Article 112.- The Industrial Integration Programs and Projects shall provide for exclusive benefits and effective preferential treatment for Bolivia and Ecuador to help them take effective advantage of the subregional market.

Article 113.- The General Secretariat, in proposing to the Commission the complementary measures envisaged in Article 69, shall provide for exclusive advantages and preferential treatment for Bolivia and Ecuador, when necessary.

The Commission, at the General Secretariat's proposal, shall take the measures that are necessary to ensure that the allocations granted to Bolivia and Ecuador are effective and fully utilized, particularly those aimed at strengthening commitments in respect to the allocations made to those countries, to the extension of the time periods for maintaining the allocations, and to the execution of the projects assigned to them under the Industrial Development Programs.

Section C - On Trade Policy

Article 114.- The corrective measures referred to in Articles 90 and 96 shall be extended to imports from Bolivia and Ecuador only in duly qualified cases and when the General Secretariat has been able to ascertain that the serious adverse effects stem substantially from those imports. In this case, the General Secretariat shall observe the procedures stipulated in Articles 91 and 96 and the regulations adopted by the Commission at the General Secretariat's proposal with respect to the corresponding safeguard provisions.

Article 115.- The General Secretariat shall give special and priority attention, in the cooperation efforts to which Article 69 refers, to the industries of Bolivia and Ecuador whose products are excluded by those countries from their Liberalization Programs, in order to help equip them to participate in the subregional market as rapidly as possible.

Section D - On The Common External Tariff

Article 116.- Bolivia and Ecuador shall begin the process of adopting the Common External Tariff on an annual, automatic, and linear basis, on the date set by the Commission.

Bolivia and Ecuador shall be required to adopt the Common Minimum External Tariff for products that are not produced in the Subregion, as referred to in Article 80. They shall adopt the minimum customs duties for those products through a linear and automatic process that shall be completed three years after the date on which these products are first produced in the Subregion.

The stipulations of the first paragraph of this Article notwithstanding, the Commission, at the proposal of the General Secretariat, may determine that Bolivia and Ecuador should adopt the minimum tariff levels for products of interest to the other Member Countries, provided that the application of those levels is not detrimental to Bolivia or Ecuador.

The Commission, based on the evaluations referred to in Article 131, shall determine the procedure and timeframe for the adoption of the Common Minimum External Tariff by Bolivia and Ecuador. In any case, the Commission shall bear in mind the problems deriving from Bolivia's landlocked situation referred to in Article 4 of this Agreement.

The Commission may also, at the General Secretariat's proposal, determine that Bolivia and Ecuador should adopt the minimum tariff levels for products whose importation from outside of the subregion may cause serious problems for the Subregion.

In drawing up its proposals on the Common External Tariff, the General Secretariat shall bear in mind the provisions of Article 4 benefiting Bolivia.

Article 117.- Bolivia and Ecuador may establish the exceptions authorized by the Commission, at the General Secretariat's proposal, to the alignment of their national tariff schedules with the Common External Tariff, to enable them to apply their existing industrial development laws, mainly with respect to the importation of the capital goods, intermediate goods, and raw materials they need for their development.

Those exceptions may not be applied in any case more than two years before the Common External Tariff is fully implemented.

Section E - On Financial Cooperation and Technical Assistance

Article 118.- The Member Countries commit themselves to act jointly to secure technical assistance and financing for Bolivia and Ecuador's development needs, particularly for projects related to the integration process, from the Andean Development Corporation and any other subregional, national, or international organizations.

The resources for those projects shall be allocated in accordance with the basic objective of reducing the existing differences in development among the countries by making an attempt to favor Bolivia and Ecuador markedly.

The Member Countries, moreover, shall jointly request the Andean Development Corporation to allocate its regular and special resources in such a way that Bolivia and Ecuador are given a substantially larger share than they would receive if the distribution were to be proportional to their contribution to the Corporation's capital.

Section F - General Provisions

Article 119.- In its periodic evaluations and annual reports, the General Secretariat shall give separate and special consideration to Bolivia and Ecuador's situation in the subregional integration effort and shall propose to the Commission the measures that it deems appropriate to substantially improve their possibilities for development and increasingly expedite their participation in the area's industrialization.

Article 120.- The Commission may establish, for the benefit of any of the relatively less developed countries, more favorable conditions and procedures than those considered in this Chapter, in the light of the degree of development attained and the conditions for taking advantage of the benefits of integration.

CHAPTER XVI
ECONOMIC AND SOCIAL COOPERATION

Article 121.- Member Countries may undertake programs and measures in the area of economic and social cooperation, which shall be coordinated within the Commission and shall be limited to the spheres of competence established in this Agreement.

Article 122.- Member Countries shall undertake external efforts on matters of common interest, for the purpose of improving their participation in the international economy.

Article 123.- With respect to the provisions of the previous Article, the Andean Council of Foreign Ministers and the Commission shall, within their respective areas of jurisdiction, adopt programs to direct the joint external actions of the Member Countries, particularly as regards the negotiations with third countries and groups of countries in the political, social and economic and trade spheres, as well as their participation in forums and organizations specialized in international economic matters.

Article 124.- Member Countries shall promote a joint scientific and technological development process to attain the following objectives:

a) The creation of a subregional capacity to respond to the challenges of the scientific-technological revolution that is underway;

b) The contribution of science and technology to the conception and execution of Andean development strategies and programs; and

c) The utilization of economic integration mechanisms to incentivize technological innovation and the modernization of production.

Article 125.- For purposes of the previous Article, the Member Countries shall adopt in the fields where there is a community interest:

a) Programs of cooperation and coordinated efforts in science and technology in areas where it is more effective to train human resources and to obtain results from research at the subregional level;

b) Technological development programs that shall help to obtain solutions to common problems in the production sectors, particularly those aimed at enhancing the competitiveness of the different production sectors; and

c) Programs for taking advantage of the enlarged market and of joint physical, human, and financial capacities, in order to boost technological development in sectors of community interest.

Article 126.- The Member Countries shall undertake actions to promote the comprehensive development of border regions and their effective incorporation in the national and subregional Andean economies.

Article 127.- The Member Countries shall conduct joint tourism programs designed to gain a better understanding of the subregion and to encourage economic activities connected with this sector.

Article 128.- The Member Countries shall undertake joint actions to make better use of their renewable and non-renewable natural resources and ensure the conservation and improvement of the environment.

Article 129.- The Member Countries shall make joint cooperative efforts to help attain the following social development objectives of the Andean people:

a) Elimination of poverty among the marginalized classes, in order to achieve social justice;

b) Strengthening of the cultural identity and formation of citizenship values for the integration of the Andean subregion;

c) Full participation by the subregion's inhabitants in the integration process; and

d) Attention to the needs of the predominantly rural depressed areas.

Programs and projects shall be carried out in the areas of health, social security, low-cost housing, education, and culture, in order to attain such objectives.

The various organizations of the Andean system shall coordinate the actions that are taken pursuant to this Article.

Article 130.- For the purposes indicated in the previous article, the respective Ministers of the social areas, meeting as an Enlarged Commission, shall adopt the following in the fields of community interest:

a) Educational programs aimed at renewing and improving the quality of basic education;

b) Programs that seek to diversify and improve the technical level and coverage of the professional training and job training systems;

c) Programs aimed at securing the recognition of higher educational degrees at the Andean level, in order to facilitate the provision of professional services in the subregion;

d) People's participation programs oriented toward bringing about the full incorporation of the rural and semi-rural areas in the development process.

e) Programs to promote social support systems and projects, aimed at promoting the participation of small enterprises and of networks of microenterprises and associative enterprises, interlinked within the enlarged economic space;

f) Programs for promoting initiatives aimed at the protection and well-being of the working population; and

g) Policy harmonization programs in the fields of women's participation in economic activity; of child and family protection and support; and of attention to the ethnic groups and local communities.

Article 131.- The Member Countries shall take measures in the area of social communication and action oriented toward disseminating a fuller understanding of the subregion's cultural, historical, and geographic heritage, the economic and social situation of the subregion, and the Andean integration process.

Article 132.- The projects, measures, and programs to which this Chapter refers shall be carried out simultaneously and in coordination with the perfecting of the other mechanisms of the subregional integration process.

CHAPTER XVII
ADHERENCE, EFFECTIVE DATE AND DENOUNCEMENT

Article 133.- This Agreement may not be signed with reservations and shall remain open to the adherence of the rest of the Latin American countries. The relatively less economically developed countries that adhere to the Agreement shall be entitled to a treatment similar to that agreed upon in Chapter XV for Bolivia and Ecuador.

The Commission shall define the terms of adherence, bearing in mind that the incorporation of new members must comply with the objectives of the Agreement.

Article 134.- This Agreement shall become effective when all of the Member Countries that sign it have deposited their respective instruments of ratification with the Andean Community General Secretariat.

This Agreement may not be signed with reservations and shall have an indefinite duration.

Article 135.- Any Member Country wishing to denounce this Agreement shall so inform the Commission. From that moment on it shall cease to enjoy the rights and have the obligations deriving from its status as a Member, with the exception of the benefits received and granted in accordance with the Subregional Liberalization Program, which shall remain effective for a period of five years after the date of the denouncement.

The time period stipulated in the paragraph above may be shortened in duly substantiated cases by decision of the Commission and at the request of the interested Member Country.

Insofar as the Industrial Integration Programs are concerned, the stipulation of Article 62 paragraph i) shall be applied.

CHAPTER XVIII
ASSOCIATE MEMBERS

Article 136.- The Andean Council of Foreign Ministers meeting in enlarged session may, at the proposal of the Andean Commission, with the interested country having expressed its will, confer the status of Associate Member on a country that has entered into a free trade agreement with the Andean Community Member Countries.

Article 137.- Upon granting a country the status of Associate Member, the Andean Council of Foreign Ministers and the Andean Community Commission shall, in keeping with their respective spheres of competence and after having heard the opinion of the General Secretariat, define the following through the adoption of a Decision:

a) The bodies and institutions of the Andean Integration System to which the Associate Country shall belong, together with the terms for its participation;

b) The mechanisms and measures of the Cartagena Agreement in which the Associate Member Country shall participate; and

c) The provisions that shall be applied to the relations between the Associate Member Country and the rest of the Member Countries, as well as the way those relations shall be administered.

The aspects provided for in this article may be revised at any time, in keeping with the procedures and spheres of competence stipulated herein.

CHAPTER XIX
FINAL PROVISIONS

Article 138.-The Commission, at the proposal of the General Secretariat, and based upon the latter's periodic reports and evaluations, shall adopt the necessary mechanisms to ensure the attainment of the objectives of the Agreement once the process of trade liberalization and establishment of the Common External Tariff has concluded. Those mechanisms must provide for special treatment favoring Bolivia and Ecuador so long as the present differences in degree of development continue to exist.

Article 139.- Any advantage, favor, exemption, immunity, or privilege that is applied by a Member Country to a product originating in or destined for any other country, shall be immediately and unconditionally extended to the similar product originating in or destined for the territory of the other Member Countries.

Advantages, favors, exemptions, immunities, and privileges already granted or to be granted by virtue of agreements among Member Countries or between Member Countries and third countries, for the purpose of facilitating border traffic, shall be excepted from the treatment referred to in the previous paragraph.

CHAPTER XX
TEMPORARY PROVISIONS

First.- The stipulations of Article 76 of the Cartagena Agreement notwithstanding, the Andean Community Commission shall define the terms of the Liberalization Program to be applied to the trade between Peru and the rest of the Member Countries, with a view to having the Andean Free Trade Area fully operational by December 31, 2005 at the latest. Peru shall not be obliged to apply the Common External Tariff until the Commission decides on the timeframes and ways and means for Peru's incorporation in this mechanism.

Second.- The Member Countries shall provisionally apply the stipulations of the Chapter on Associate Members and the First Temporary Provision until the ratification procedures required by their respective national laws have been completed.

Third.- The Andean Community Commission may establish an arbitrational mechanism to settle disputes among Member Countries that extend beyond the General Secretariat's decision.

Fourth.- Alterations in the tariff level resulting from Ecuador's conversion of its National Customs Tariff due to the adoption of the Brussels Tariff Nomenclature, are excepted from the stipulations of Article 77.

Fifth.- The Commission may situate the products covered by Decision 120, once it has been derogated, in any of the modes of the Liberalization Program; it may also add them to the new reserve list referred to in the Second Temporary Provision.

ANNEX I

1. To delegate to the General Secretariat the attributions it deems advisable.

2. To approve the draft amendments to this Agreement.

3. To amend the General Secretariat's proposals.

4. To approve the provisions that are needed to make it possible to coordinate the development plans and harmonize the economic policies of the Member Countries.

5. To approve the provisions and define the timeframes for gradually harmonizing the Member Countries´ instruments to regulate foreign trade.

6. To approve the physical integration programs.

7. To accelerate the Liberalization Program, by products or product groups.

8. To approve the joint agricultural and agroindustrial development programs, by products or product groups.

9. To approve and modify the list of agricultural products to which Article 92 refers.

10. To approve the measures for joint cooperation established in Article 96.

11. To approve, not approve, or amend Member Country proposals.

12. To reduce the number of subject matters included in this Annex.

13. To establish the terms for adherence to this Agreement.

14. To approve the Common External Tariff in accordance with the modes provided for in Chapter VIII, establish the terms for its application and modify the common tariff levels.

15. To approve the measures referred to in the last paragraph of Article 91.

ANNEX II

1. To approve the terms for the incorporation for non-participant Member Countries in the Industrial Integration Programs.

2. To approve the list of products that are not produced in any country of the Subregion.

3. To approve the special rules of origin.

Index

Selected Bibliography

And where do we begin? Priorities of the Andean Community regarding Climate Change. Lima, Peru: General Secretary of the Andean Community, the United Nations Program for the Environment, Regional Office for Latin America and the Caribbean and the Spanish Agency for International Cooperation, 2007, 37.

Andean Community. General Secretariat. '*28 Years of Andean Integration. An Historical Recount*', 8.

Andean Community website: www.comunidadandina.org, Infrastructure and borders.

Andean Community website: www.comunidadandina.org, Subregional Regulations.

Andean Informative, No. 9, May 1996 (*Andean Newsletter*).

Andean Informative No. 11 (*Andean Newsletter*).

The Constitutive Agreement of the CAF (July 1999); CAF, '*30 Years of Support to Integration and Sustainable Development*' (CAF, August 2000) website: www.caf.com

Declaration of the VII Andean Social Development Ministers Council, 6 July 2011.

Integrated Social Development Plan, Decision 601, Extraordinary Meeting of the Andean Council of Foreign Affairs Ministers, 21 September 2004.

Maldonado Lira, Héctor. *30 Years of Andean Integration Balance and Perspective.* Lima, Peru: Andean Community. General Secretariat, 1999, 97, 112.

Regional Biodiversity Strategy for the Countries in the Andean Tropic, Executive Summary, 3.

Salgado, Germánico. '*Ecuador and the Economic Integration of Latin America*' in *Labor Policy in the Andean Group*, ed. Luis Aparicio Valdez. BID-INTAL, 177.

Study for a program of actions for the union and convergence among the different schemes of integration. Document prepared for the ALADI/CEPAL/SELA meeting of the government officials responsible for the commercial policy of Latin America and the Caribbean (Quito, Ecuador, 10–11 October 1994).

Valdez, Luis Aparicio & Morgado V. Emilio. *Study on Andean Socio-Labor Integration. Specially the Simon Rodriguez Agreement.* Lima, Peru: ANALISIS LABORAL, May 1999.

Vieira Posada, Edgard. *The Extended Andean Market: A Reality.* Colombia: Chamber of Commerce of Bogota, April 1999, 24, 27.

Website of the Latin American Reserve Fund: www.flar.net

Index

The numbers here refer to paragraph numbers.

Made in the USA
Monee, IL
18 October 2026

66037595R10085